Steward of Stories

Steward of Stories

Reflecting on Tensions in Daily Discipleship

JOANN A. POST

RESOURCE *Publications* · Eugene, Oregon

STEWARD OF STORIES
Reflecting on Tensions in Daily Discipleship

Copyright © 2014 JoAnn A. Post. All rights reserved. Except for brief quotations in critical publications or reviews, no part of this book may be reproduced in any manner without prior written permission from the publisher. Write: Permissions, Wipf and Stock Publishers, 199 W. 8th Ave., Suite 3, Eugene, OR 97401.

Resource Publications
An Imprint of Wipf and Stock Publishers
199 W. 8th Ave., Suite 3
Eugene, OR 97401

www.wipfandstock.com

ISBN 13: 978-1-62564-673-6

Manufactured in the U.S.A.

05/10/2014

For Sis and Squeak

Contents

A First Word ix

Acknowledgments xiii

Pastoral Life

1. Call Me 3
2. Your Secret Is Safe 12
3. This Far, and No Farther 21
4. May I Come In? 29
5. I Don't Know Your Life 37
6. Time to Go 45

Congregational Life

7. Can You Hear Me Now? 57
8. The Little Dunker 66
9. Two or Three 75
10. Happy Family 83
11. Hitching Horses 90
12. Last Gasp 99
13. Miss Mary 107
14. We Are Not Worthy 113

Contents

Daily Life

15	Still Known	123
16	Not a Prayer	129
17	Marry Me?	137
18	Sincerely Dead	146
	A Last Word	155
	Bibliography	157

A First Word

In one hot Iowa summer almost forty years ago, I devoured all four volumes of James Herriot's *All Creatures Great and Small* series, and Truman Capote's *In Cold Blood*. Dr. Herriot mused on decades of veterinary practice in the rolling hills of Yorkshire, England. Mr. Capote chronicled the brutal slayings of a Kansas farm family by drifters in search of easy money. As I lay reading in the boughs of the sprawling maple behind the farmhouse, I recognized the farm yards and fertile fields in which Dr. Herriot labored, and the endless rolling Kansas landscape on which Mr. Capote's tale of true terror unfolded. Even as an adolescent, I wondered at the environs that could spawn both bucolic serenity and bone-chilling horror. An outsider to the rural life would have to conclude that either Dr. Herriot's depiction was pure fantasy or Mr. Capote's obscene anomaly. But both stories were true. The same pastoral vista on which lambs frolic and mares graze once stood witness to the absolute depravity of human nature.

Like the rich earth that provokes both musing memoir and heinous history, the Lutheran parishes I have served have given rise to both wise counsel and desperate action on my part. The landscape of my ministry, while geographically diverse, has provoked questions and dilemmas unique only in the details, otherwise common to all in this calling.

My husband has dubbed me "Steward of Stories," as both strangers and friends invite me into their lives, and entrust their secret hopes and public nightmares, their much-loved personal narratives with me. It is my intent to steward these stories well, to honor those who have called me "Pastor," as well as those whose lives have brushed past mine in silent, but significant ways.

In three decades of parish ministry, I have been privileged to hear thousands of stories, and to serve wonderfully ordinary parishes from Alaska to Georgia to Wisconsin to Connecticut. In each of four congregations and in a campus ministry setting, I have baptized babies and confirmed teenagers and married thirty-somethings and buried the elderly. I have also baptized the elderly and confirmed thirty-somethings and married teenagers and buried babies. This life is rich with contradictions and conundrums, teeming with challenges and choices, humbling in its privileges and perspectives.

Here is the paradox of the pastor's reality, a life immersed in life's joys and sorrows into which few but the pastor (and the country veterinarian) are invited. The pastor holds wet wrinkled newborns and the dry papery hands of the aged. The pastor receives more love than anyone deserves, and labors under more criticism than is warranted. The same action is praised by some and scorned by others. The pastor is called to preach the Holy Word of God, and find the ordinary word that prevents Congregation Meeting mutiny. The pastor offers forgiveness to the sinner who refuses to receive it. The pastor earns a congregation's trust when these competing demands, these impossible expectations are faithfully and wisely negotiated. And, because of that trust, the pastor is then invited into deeper conversations, darker moments, and (appropriately) intimate relationship.

We called it The Pickle, the faded green 1994 Ford Taurus station wagon my friends drove until the air conditioning was in no condition, and the windows preferred "half-mast" to either open or closed. They dubbed the rear cargo space the "way back." Groceries went in the "way back," as did dogs, bicycles, crumpled McDonald's bags, and the annoying neighbor child who didn't really merit a seatbelt. My "ministry memory" is just such a way back, cluttered with snippets of song lyrics and dirty jokes, the wilted leaves of wincing memories, sorrows sensitive to touch, poignant moments that still reduce me to tears. Every once in a while some crumpled scrap of wisdom tumbles out of the pile and I am glad I didn't throw it out.

From this "way back" of my ministry memory, I have retrieved deceivingly simple stories that draw the reader into reflection about the pastor's life, the congregation's life, and the life of the faithful. In each of these narratives, I pair pastoral experiences that reveal the conundrums present in daily parish ministry. Why did one stillbirth result in a naming, and another in a baptism? How is the concept of "family" an inspiring descriptor in one congregation, and a trap in another? Is it possible for a single congregation to be both deeply hospitable and tightly closed? While it is true that some things are simply right and others are simply wrong, it is more often true that the demands of the moment, the particulars of a situation,

A First Word

the pressures of time, can make decisions about "right and wrong" luxuries which neither time nor circumstance afford. Years of parish practice have helped me to make peace with the changes and chances of this life, to release my death grip on "being right," to trust God's wisdom and that of fellow disciples.

The competing demands presented by the pastoral life are challenging to even a seasoned pastor. But when the unexpected or unwelcome presents itself to the newly ordained, the new pastor lies awake nights worrying about doing the "right thing." When congregational lay leaders are forced to face a hard truth, a reality that slices through the canvas of their carefully painted self-portrait, it is often easier to flee than to face it. I think of these demands as "competing faithfulnesses": the daily tension between faithfulness to scripture and tradition, to the people we are called to serve and to our additional callings as parents and spouses and children, friends and neighbors and colleagues. To whom or what do we owe the highest faithfulness? Which of these competing faithfulnesses emerges as the greatest? When do we appeal to pastoral authority, the "because I said so," answer, and when do we bite our tongues and wait for the word, for the wisdom, for the way through?

I write for seminary professors and students, parish pastors and congregational lay leaders, teachers and students who, like me, struggle to live and understand the life of faith. As I have shared my work with each of these audiences, they have heard questions that may have nipped at their own heels but have previously gone unarticulated or unanswered. They are grateful for the realization that there might be more than one "right" way to approach parish ministry. They are fascinated by the intricacies of this work that, on the face of it, is so straightforward. Like me, they are relieved to have an opportunity to speak honestly about failure and forgiveness, undeserved grace and tender mercy.

All of the stories in this collection are real and happened to me. Out of respect for those involved, names and details, locations, circumstances and identifying marks have been altered. When a story is very specific, I have consulted those involved. Most characters and events are composites, an amalgam of individual encounters that illustrate a common experience. In every circumstance, especially those in which I was at odds with others, I seek to portray their views and actions in the most charitable light. There are, of course, stories from my ministry which will never appear in print. Some stories are so painful, so personal, so sensitive that they will go with

A First Word

me to my grave. I am deeply grateful to the congregations and individuals whose lives and stories have informed my ministry, who have shaped me as a pastor and a person. I trust these essays will be seen not as broken confidence, but as gifts to our shared ministry, opportunities to recognize ourselves in disciples from across the church.

Through the mash-up of stories from my own ministry, readers are invited into conversation about their own ministry settings in a more subtle way than to simply say, "Let's talk about sacramental practice," or "Power is a problem here." I find that it is much easier to discuss ministry dilemmas if that dilemma is presented by someone else, in a setting different from one's own. With my narrative reflections as a foot in the door, these essays may prompt reflection on the difficulties and opportunities facing those in parish ministry. Ideally, these essays open a safe entrance to discussion of their own ministry settings. Additionally, each is accompanied by questions to focus the discussion of the ministry matter at hand.

However, more than enabling simple storytelling among colleagues and in congregations, I write to draw me and my readers closer to God. God is not merely an idea, a concept to be studied. We believe God has chosen to be known through Jesus Christ, taking on human likeness. We are the stewards of God's story in the world, a story both ancient and still-being-written. It is among the people we are privileged to serve, in the congregations which are part of the Body of Christ, that we know God most fully. As each essay unfolds, I hope to open the reader to new and provocative experiences of God at work in each of us.

Dr. Herriot and Mr. Capote wrote of like landscapes on which unlike events unfolded. I write of a single landscape, as well, the landscape of parish ministry. On that familiar landscape, congregations filled with wise and foolish disciples stumble and stride, dance and drudge through the ministries to which we have been called. I introduce you to these, my colleagues and congregations, trusting that you will find yourself among them and more important, find God at work in you.

Acknowledgments

Much of the writing for this collection took place during a sabbatical leave which turned into extended medical disability leave for treatment of cancer. On those days when the effects of chemotherapy didn't interfere, I relished uninterrupted hours to write and to reflect on my life as a parish pastor. Though isolated by illness and fragility, writing about the congregations and people I love kept me in community with them, and made the months of confinement less arduous.

I am first and deeply indebted to them, the congregations of which it has been my privilege to be a pastor. In each case, the people with whom I serve have given far more than they received. I thank them for entrusting their lives and their stories to me.

Writing workshops at the Collegeville Institute for Ecumenical Research, and a Pastoral Study Grant from the Louisville Institute afforded time to write and to think apart from the daily demands of work and family. I was the grateful recipient of a Lilly Endowment National Clergy Renewal Grant, which funded a three-month sabbatical to create a space for writing.

Reading groups in Coon Rapids, Iowa; Walla Walla, Washington; and Manchester, Connecticut field tested a number of these essays and provided valuable insight.

My clergy colleague group indulged me by discussing some of these essays at our monthly gatherings.

My book club allowed me to intersperse an essay here and there among the "real" books we discussed at our monthly meetings.

Dorothy Bass and Craig Dykstra each read the manuscript, and prodded me to pursue publication.

Jan Boden, my copyeditor, brought precision and clarity to the project.

I am grateful for and still surprised by the confidence placed in me by the staff at Wipf and Stock.

Acknowledgments

The oldest essay in this collection, "Still Known," has its roots in a letter I wrote to my professor and friend Herbert Anderson. Herbert still carries that letter with him. I carry his pastoral wisdom and enduring friendship with me everywhere I go, as well.

Two friends have been with me from the first word to the last. My trusted ministry colleague Joel Ley helped pair stories for these essays, and craft the discussion questions that follow each essay. My sister Mary Bower provided technical advice and theological insight from her own vantage point as a seasoned editor and as a faithful congregational leader.

For thirty years, my favorite reader and advisor has been my beloved husband, James. He not only read these stories, but lived them with me. For the stories we have already shared, and all the chapters yet to be written, I am humbled and grateful.

Pastoral Life

1

Call Me

It was a brilliant spring day, the first day we could open the windows of the church office. I had barely finished wiping up winter's dust from the window sills, when the phone rang. I paid no attention. Most phone calls were for the parish secretary and not for me. I often kidded that I was the hood ornament on the car that was that congregation.

Donna buzzed me on the intercom. "A 'Jeb' on the phone for you. He says you'll be glad to hear from him." Assuming it was a telemarketer feigning familiarity, I answered with a note of dismissive disdain in my voice. "This is Pastor Post." He laughed through the phone, a wonderful throaty guffaw that I would know anywhere. "Hey it's me! It's Jeb! How are you?"

I had not spoken with Jeb in the years since I had left my last parish. He had been an active lay leader, an anchoring baritone in the church choir, a well-respected community leader. He was a wonderful man. Just hearing his voice made me smile.

We gleefully caught up on the gossip about our families and work and church, and then he said, "Here's why I'm calling."

The senior pastor of that parish—a much-loved, hardworking pastor who had led the parish into courageous ministry ventures—was retiring. Jeb was the chair of the call committee. He said, "JoAnn, you know Pastor Joss is retiring. We're looking to call a senior pastor who is a powerful preacher, a strong administrator, a real community leader. Pastor's shoes will be hard to fill, but we're in a really strong position right now. We think the next pastor will have a ball. But it needs to be someone special."

As he was speaking, rehearsing the qualifications needed in the next senior pastor, I was already trying to figure out how to let him down easily.

I was happy in my call. My husband's work was satisfying. My family was settled. We were not looking to move. As Jeb continued, I adopted a pitying attitude, much like when the most popular girl in the class turns down a date with the nerdiest boy. Of course they would want to put my name on their short list. Who wouldn't? But I couldn't. I would have to let Jeb down easily.

I was barely listening anymore, flattered at the attention, already crafting the story for telling at the supper table, when he paused. "JoAnn, this is a big call that needs just the right person. Do you know anybody?"

What? Jeb wasn't asking me to the prom. He wondered if I had a cute friend.

Since being ordained in 1985, I have been in five call processes—four for parish calls and a fifth for campus ministry. In each case, I entered the process with trembling knees and dry mouth. And, in each case, the calls were to places I swore I would never go.

When my husband and I graduated from seminary and were seeking our first parish calls, we asked to be assigned to the North Pacific District of the American Lutheran Church (ALC) (neither entity exists any longer). It was my husband's home turf and a wonderful place to live. We said we would gladly serve anywhere in the district's five-state region. Anywhere but Alaska. Who wanted to go to Alaska? Cold. Desolate. Distant. There were more polar bears than Lutherans on that godforsaken tundra. Fortunately, both the district president and God ignored our well-reasoned, warm-blooded restrictions, and we each served wonderful calls in Anchorage—calls that changed the course of our professional and personal lives.

When my husband decided to pursue doctoral work in theology, we opened ourselves to a wide array of academic institutions. I was willing to go anywhere. Except Atlanta. Hot. Sweaty. Far from home. I was not interested in learning to drawl or drink sweet tea or spend afternoons fanning myself on the front porch. Fortunately, both the synod bishop and God ignored my small-minded, Yankee-centric objections and I served as associate pastor in a diverse, challenging, lively parish in midtown Atlanta while my husband pursued his PhD.

As my husband's graduate studies drew to a close, and we turned our attention to seeking an academic position for him, I said I was willing to go anywhere. Except Iowa. Don't get me wrong. I am a proud Iowa native, product of Iowa's world-recognized educational system. Most of my family lives there. I still get misty-eyed when I think of the whisper of corn leaves on hot summer nights, the pumpkin-orange harvest moons of autumn, the barren snow-covered fields in winter, the only-in-Iowa tender green of spring leaves. Iowa leads the nation in education and agriculture and social change. But, with all due respect, it's Iowa. Once you've seen one pig, you've seen them all. Fortunately, a seminary board, two call committees and God ignored my whining, and, in our thirteen-year sojourn there, I served two wonderful calls while my husband taught at our denominational seminary.

At some point, you would think I would pay attention to the pattern. But each time I said, "Hell, no, I won't go," God sent me there. And each time, I experienced hospitality and challenge, growth and friendship beyond any expectations, in spite of my pouty biases.

When our older daughter graduated from high school and our younger daughter was still in grade school, we saw a window of opportunity. If we were going to move again, that was the time. "Anywhere you want to go," I said out loud to my husband, silently in prayer to God. And this time I meant it. So we went.

We moved to New England, a delightful place, but, to be honest, not among my Top Ten Destinations. When I first met with the bishop of the New England Synod, I said, "I'm ready for a new challenge." She laughed a diabolical bishop's laugh and slid a file folder across the table at me. "I don't know if we'd be sending you there to close the doors or fling them open." After a whirlwind courtship, the parish called and I accepted. To this day, both failure and full life are real possibilities there. But I am so grateful to have had the privilege of serving a congregation where the Spirit was so visibly at work, blowing doors open, airing out stuffy corners, sometimes lifting us right off our feet.

A parish pastor is *called*. Not hired. Not placed. Not appointed. A parish pastor is *called*. The choice of language for this vocational critter is critical. To be called is to place oneself in the "wind tunnel of the Spirit." To be called is to open oneself to the needs of the larger church and the peculiarities of a particular community of faith. To be called is to trust that, however outlandish or improbable the match, God might be at work in the making.

So what does it mean to be "called?" And how do we know a particular call is of God, and not a foolish whim or a random circumstance or stubborn foot-planting or vain pride or a confusion of God's voice with the other voices in my head?

Pastoral Life

There are lots of practical considerations. Pastors are not immune from the concerns that all working people have. Can the pastor afford to live in that community? Is there work for a spouse, good schools for children? Is it near enough extended family? Is there a parsonage or will the pastor have to buy her own home? Does the congregation care about the things the pastor cares about?

And then there are the intangibles, variables which differ pastor to pastor. In my experience, I know an opportunity to be a "call" when my heart skips a beat, when my palms get sweaty, when I can't sleep at night for imagining the possibilities. It's not every pastor's critical sign, but it works for me. Of course, before I get to the giddy "falling in love" stage, God has always already done all the heavy lifting of getting me to consider a call at all.

This is not to say that a pastor makes foolish decisions, or throws caution to the wind, or ignores important evidence. The pastor must find that tender place between analysis paralysis and dreamland.

The order for installing pastors in parish settings includes the haunting question, "Do you believe that the call of the church is the call of God?" I have learned to say, with only a little hesitation, "Yes." After all, who but God would have pulled us from one coast to another, into wildly different ministry settings among people whose culture and expectations were foreign to us? Who but God would have taken such care in both the uprooting and the replanting? The parishes I have served have pulled out every ounce of courage, humility, patience, and hope I have, and I am a better pastor for the pulling. To quote the psalmist, "This is God's doing. It is wonderful in our eyes" (Ps 118:23).

I am by nature stubborn and smarter than everybody else on the planet. But time after time, God has been proven smarter and more stubborn than I. Time after time, I have had to mutter those three little words that God loves to hear, "You were right." I imagine I'll mutter them again a time or two before I retire.

At the risk of sharing too much information, I have to admit that my third call, a part-time call to campus ministry, was taken for less than holy or heart-pounding reasons. I used it, in part, for my own mercenary ends.

When we married, my husband and I had hoped to have a large family—as many children as we could churn out. But after the birth of our older daughter, we were plagued with infertility issues. Our private lives were overrun with doctors and tests and thermometers and tears. When my husband accepted a call to teach at a seminary and I knew I would be seeking a new call, we decided that I should work part-time. After all, parish ministry is stressful and stress can't be good for a woman desiring to be pregnant. I was advised to slow down, take a step back, concentrate on being healthy and hopeful. Surely, if I worked a little less and ran a little slower, my closed womb would be opened and children would fall from the sky (or wherever children come from).

I enjoyed the pace of campus ministry far more than I expected. Ministry with students is a blast. There was always something happening on campus. The campus ministry was a respected part of both the campus and town communities. Local pastors included the campus pastor in all their events. (Weekends were free.) It was an ideal setting for a pastor who wanted to get pregnant. Certainly, I missed the rhythm of parish ministry—weekly preaching and seasonal liturgies and regular contact with a broad range of ages and circumstances. I missed leg hugs from toddlers and dry kisses from old ladies, coffee with the old guys and even late-night council meetings. But I kept reminding myself that my full-time call was to get pregnant, so part-time ministry was okay. For now.

When the pastor at the Lutheran parish nearest the campus took a call to another congregation, I was encouraged to consider the possibility of serving as pastor there. It was a great congregation, full of kids and energy, music and hope. A parade of students and faculty supplemented the folks who had been members there for generations. We used their facility for campus ministry events; many of the students worshipped there; it was a plum of a parish. I liked them. They liked me.

However, a return to full-time parish ministry was not in The Plan. I was trying to relax. I was trying to be healthy. I was doing everything in my power to get pregnant. As a courtesy to the chair of the call committee, I submitted my paper work and allowed myself to be considered for the call. But I knew they would be interviewing candidates far more suited than I. And I knew that my first priority was fertility, not full-time work, so I curbed my enthusiasm.

They did, in fact, interview a number of wonderful pastoral candidates. I knew them all, and knew that any one of them would serve the parish well. It was a relief to me that the candidate pool was so deep—the congregation would call one of those pastors and I would be off the hook.

I was so convinced that another of the candidates was the right one, that I spent a good portion of an out-of-town conference the following week writing a letter removing myself from the call process. While speakers droned on and on, as motions were made and passed and defeated, I scribbled a letter on a borrowed legal pad. The letter was actually a long list of reasons I was not a good candidate, reasons they should extend the call to someone else. It was a relief to write the letter, to put an end to the wondering. My mind was made up.

During a coffee break, I stopped by my hotel room to grab a stick of gum from my purse and saw the red "message" light on the phone blinking. (These events occurred long before the advent of cell phones and unlimited access.) I had missed a phone call from the chair of the call committee at the parish back home: "Call as soon as you can."

I sat down on the edge of the bed, knowing that he would not have tracked me down at a conference halfway across the country to tell me no. Before returning his call, I reviewed my scribbled notes, called my husband, cried a prayer for wisdom, and said "no" out loud several times for practice. When the call committee chair heard my voice on the phone, he said. "JoAnn, the call committee met last night. You are our unanimous choice to serve as our next pastor. Will you accept?" I sighed and said, "Yes."

"Do you believe that the call of the church is the call of God?" This is more than a perfunctory question.

Pastors are in a unique position to be responsible to both a particular congregation and the larger church. The pastor is called to respect a time-tested congregational system and to dismantle it for the sake of emerging ministry. The pastor is called to respect the wisdom and ways of a congregation's elders, and to draw in new people with new ideas. The pastor is to steward the congregation's financial stability, and to take risks for the sake of the Gospel. The pastor is to teach and learn, speak and be silent, lead and follow, challenge and acquiesce. The pastor is servant of all and servant of God alone.

Parish ministry is not a job. It is a calling—a calling that only a starstruck fool would consider. I am one of those fools. Happily so.

But how do you know when the congregation's call is of God? There is no magic. No writing on the wall. No fail-safe method for discerning. The pastor calls on the wisdom of trusted friends and advisors. She is honest about her skills and passions, and her failings and faults. The pastor listens carefully to what the calling congregation says and what they really mean. The pastor prays and chews fingernails and studies documents and follows her heart. Like I said, only a fool . . .

I am curious to know how people who are not pastors think about their work, discern new opportunities, balance practicality with passion.

Here's an example. My extended family farms; it's all we have ever done and I am intensely proud of them. I often boast that my family feeds the world. Farming, like parish ministry, is a completely consuming vocation. But do farmers farm because it makes their hearts sing, or because the investment of time and money makes a shift of vocation impossible? What of teachers? And store clerks? And governors? And stay-at-home parents? And bartenders? I honestly don't know how they think about their work.

I also know that not all parish pastors are as gob smacked by the vocation as I am. To be sure, there are days when I'm tempted to drive away and never look back, but those days are few-and-far-between. I mostly love what I do. It would be worthwhile to ask other pastors how they think of the vocation, if it is a matter of a singing heart or a steady paycheck. I imagine a whole new set of conversations opening—conversations about vocation and work, satisfaction and necessity, love and duty.

I fibbed earlier when I said I had been in five call processes. In fact, there was a sixth, a process I aborted and try hard not to think about. The congregation wanted me to say yes, but I said no. It is the only time I have turned a congregation down in my life. It still haunts me.

I submitted to be interviewed by an inner city congregation, a venerable dowager of a place as full of opportunity as it was of danger. The people I met during the process were wonderful to me and deeply committed to the congregation. A lot of good things were happening there. I have rarely seen members of a parish so hopeful, so eager, so ready to roll up their sleeves. But after three days of interviews and meetings, during which they courted me and fed me and toured me and promised me the moon, I had a hole in the pit of my stomach. On the last day of my visit, just hours before the final meeting with the call committee, I climbed the steep stairs into the sanctuary's dark balcony to pray. And instead all I could do was cry. I wanted to love them. I wanted to serve them. I wanted to be the pastor they had been praying for. So why the tears?

The parish would have pressed enormous challenges on me, would have called on everything I had and a lot of things I didn't. They faced a changing ethnic neighborhood, a deteriorating city structure, a building literally falling down around their ears, a nearly empty sanctuary week after week, far more funerals than baptisms, decades of deficit budgets and a dwindling endowment. None of these are unique issues, nor were they fatal flaws. It would have been hard, exhausting, perhaps thankless work. I have never shied away from hard work or surrendered to an uphill battle. But it was not the workload that spooked me. It was that their call did not make my heart flutter.

After that evening's final call committee meeting, the chair said, "We can't do this without a congregational vote, but we want you to know we'll be recommending you to the congregation for call. Don't say anything now, but we pray you'll say 'yes' when the call comes."

Hugs and tears and meaningful handshakes followed. I bid them good night with a lump in my throat, knowing there would be no congregational call meeting. In my mind, I was writing the letter removing myself from the process before I left the building.

I realized that night, lying awake in a hotel bed, counting the hours until boarding a flight for home, that accepting a call to congregational ministry really is like falling in love. Every process before that, and every process since, has left me weak in the knees, unable to sleep for anticipation, giddy with hope and fear.

But not this one. This was not my call. I was not their pastor. Just writing these words makes my heart sad. But you can't make yourself fall in love. I couldn't accept their call.

I love parish ministry, can't imagine doing anything else. It is not a job, it is a calling. A consuming fire. An identity. A life's work. A privilege. A daily battle and a daily joy. And when parish ministry no longer makes my heart sing, no longer keeps me awake at night, I'll know it is time to do something else.

How do you know when the call of the church is the call of God? It is when they call to say "Will you?" And breathlessly you say, "I will. With the help of God. I will."

Call Me Questions for Discussion

1. What is the central dilemma portrayed in this essay?

2. If pastoral candidates must discern the suitability of a call, how does the congregation discern when a pastoral candidate is suited for that particular ministry?

3. Does the discernment of call happen only at the beginning of a ministry, or might it continue throughout the ministry?

4. Is the idea of "call" unique to pastoral ministry, or could that apply to other careers?

2

Your Secret Is Safe

It was cold on the floor. She lay there, cursing her old-lady bladder, her swollen knees, her bony butt. Not that many years ago she had been able to sleep soundly all night. But now she was lucky to get two hours of sleep before nature called, or her legs hurt, or she just woke up for no good reason. On this particular night, shuffling sleepily to the bathroom at midnight, she had snagged her gnarled yellow toenail on the edge of the rag rug in the bathroom and fell slowly, heavily to the hard tile.

Damn.

She lay there for a moment, assessing the damage. Nothing hurt. Nothing was out of place. Nothing bled. She would have called for help, but that stupid medical alert bracelet her children had forced on her was on the bedside table. Unable to rise or roll over, too late to reach the toilet, knowing no one would hear her even if she shouted, she lay on the floor in a cooling pool of urine all through that winter's night with nothing to do but think.

Martha reflected on her life—it had been good, for the most part. She had stayed in her hometown, married Walter, her high school sweetheart, taught English at the high school. She and Walter had two children together—a son and a daughter who made them proud. Though she had been fully occupied with her own life as a young wife and mother, her parents and Walter's parents had gradually grown more and more needy. Eventually, after decades of creeping dependence and the deaths of both her father and father-in-law, Martha quit her job to be a full-time caretaker for her middle-school children, her hardworking husband, and the two demanding old widows who daily held court at her kitchen table.

Martha had willingly cared for these three generations, but as a young woman she had vowed she would never do the same to her children. She would age gracefully; she would admit her weaknesses; she would let her son and daughter live their lives without being burdened by her. In short, she would be unlike every old person she knew.

But as she shivered in her damp flannel nightgown, she saw the world from another perspective, from the perspective of her children and their families. Her son and daughter took turns stopping by after work each day. They rearranged their schedules to take her to the doctor. Once a week they all came for supper, bringing the meal—and a small bottle of Manischewitz—with them. Her kids were really good to her; their spouses were like her own children. The grandchildren were wonderfully rambunctious. They didn't mind looking in on her. Or did they?

"God damn it," she thought. "I've turned into my mother."

She probably could have wiggled, crawled, or wrestled her way to a telephone, called one of the kids or maybe even dialed 911, but instead Martha forced herself to lie there in a mess of her own making until her heart agreed with the decision her mind had made.

As the winter sun dawned weakly in the window, she inched her way into the kitchen, reached for the phone high up on the wall and called her son. "David," she said. "I'm moving to the nursing home today. But could you come clean me up first? I've fallen and I can't get up."

I learned of Martha's midnight drama when David called me later that day. He and his sister, Jennifer, were feeling a little guilty for not being there when their mom fell. They also felt some guilt for the relief her decision brought. Though they loved her and would have walked over broken glass for her, Martha's care was becoming a concern. Her decision to admit herself to a care facility was an answer to a prayer they had not dared to pray. She would be safe, well-fed, surrounded by people and activity. Martha's decision meant they didn't have to make it themselves.

Surprisingly, David and Jennifer were a little afraid of how they would be regarded by the ladies in the card club, the wise guys at the coffee shop, the nosy neighbors who spent their days peeking through their living room curtains. Would they understand Martha's decision, respect them for honoring it? Or would they be accused of shelving Martha for their own convenience? I was surprised the thought of judgment had even crossed their minds. After all, there wasn't a family in town that hadn't faced similar decisions themselves. Surely, others would understand.

I was wrong.

After visiting Martha in her new digs, I decided to drop in on her dearest friend and neighbor. Martha and Jessie had been friends all their lives. They had raised their children together, had wept at their husbands' funerals together, had often commiserated about the vicissitudes and verities of old age. I knew Jessie would miss her across-the-street friend and neighbor, so I decided to stop for coffee.

I parked in the driveway of Jessie's small ranch home, and banged on the back door of the house. I called out, "It's Pastor," and let myself in. I blew cheerily into the kitchen, "How are you, Jessie? I was just at the nursing home and wanted to give you the Martha Report."

My chipper greeting was met with stony silence. Jessie wouldn't even look at me. Startled, I knelt in front of her at the kitchen table. "Jessie, what's wrong?" Slowly she turned to face me and said tightly, "She ruined it for the rest of us."

I was slow to understand Jessie's sharp judgment, but eventually it became clear to me. She was truly terrified that her own children would think Martha had done the right thing, that they might think it was time for her to leave her house, too.

"Why do you have children in the first place if they're not going to take care of you when you're old? I put up with my father until the day he died. My kids should have to put up with me." Long silence. "But now," her voice heavy with sarcasm, "Martha goes and ruins it for all the rest of us. I'm surprised my kids haven't already come to cart me away."

Later that day one of our Retired Regulars stopped by the church office to register his unsolicited opinion on Martha's move. "Those two kids never were any good. Locking their mother up in that warehouse. They should be ashamed."

Besides being mightily confused, I felt trapped. Martha had often told me she didn't want to be a burden to David and Jennifer. Her children and their families had promised to take care of her, and I had been part of conversations about what to do when they couldn't provide the care she needed. Their honest planning had been a model of good family communication. But what was I to do now, privy to these private conversations with Martha and her children? Should I defend her decision and applaud their support, or just let them twist in the wind? Did I have an obligation to publicly support them, to tell people about their careful planning, or would that be overstepping? Should I have said what I knew, or sat silently while

Martha and her children were tried in the Court of Uninformed Public Opinion?

Pastors are privileged to hear peoples' stories every day. We are told everything from the results of the most recent kindergarten progress report ("Katelynn loves to color!") to the prognosis of a recently diagnosed disease. We are invited to share the memories of the elderly, the dreams of the young, the frustration of the faltering, the shame of the sinner. The pastor is regarded as a trusted friend, a wise counselor, a silent witness.

There are, however, "levels" of confidence which a pastor must honor.

Sometimes we are told things in *confession*, as the penitent unburdens himself to the pastor, seeking God's forgiveness and mercy. Such conversations are absolutely confidential, shared with no one. The only exception to this absolute confidentiality is when someone is being harmed or will cause harm, in which case the pastor must act to protect life.

More than once I have been asked to accompany a person to the physician's or attorney's office, to listen along as hard information is shared, as decisions are made. What happens in those meetings is not confessionally confidential, but is certainly *privileged conversation*.

The *pastoral conversation* does not merit the secrecy of the confessional, the doctor's office or the attorney's conference room. Families and individuals include the pastor in their decision-making, thinking out loud in the pastor's presence, sometimes formally and other times on the fly. At the church door on Sunday morning, a member will whisper in the pastor's ear, "I'm seeing the doctor on Tuesday. I'll let you know." The couple who has suffered multiple miscarriages and pregnancy losses confides a new pregnancy to the pastor, seeking prayer and support. These conversations may not be privileged in a technical sense, but are not meant to be public, either. Such was the case with my conversations with Martha and her children.

The pastor is also privy to the *public secrets*, the information which the pastor knows, and everyone else does, too. But I have a rule for myself and for the church office—even if everyone knows, they will not have learned it from us. The pastor and church staff are not the purveyors of other peoples' information, no matter how innocuous (or juicy) the information might seem.

Pastoral Life

Let me make a brief side trip into sensitive territory. Many congregations have a prayer chain—a confidential telephone or e-mail method of inviting prayer for members and friends of the parish. In principle, a prayer chain is a good idea—what could be wrong with widening the circle of prayer? In practice, a prayer chain is a disaster waiting to happen, a burbling cesspool of gossip and unwanted intrusion. In one parish, the prayer chain was abolished when I learned that a couple of its "links" were sharing privileged prayer concerns with all their friends. In another parish, after a member invited prayer for someone who did not want his situation to be known, we had to tighten the rules to make sure the "pray-ee" was willing.

Some congregations also have the dubious practice of sharing members' health issues during the weekly announcements. Once while worshipping in another congregation on vacation, I was horrified when the pastor went on at great length in the announcements about a member's recovery from surgery. We learned about the man's blood pressure readings, his heart history, his difficulty with sleep, and how long his children had visited. I understand the desire to be supportive of those with health issues, but reading a patient's medical chart during public worship is a tremendous violation of privacy.

The introduction of electronic media and social messaging into a congregation's life presents its own unique quandary. Many people, pastors among them, have a hard time separating Facebook-appropriate communication from what would otherwise be considered gossip. It might be prudent for church staffs to have a social media policy—who posts what and when. Such caution may seem extreme, but I would rather that than endure what a colleague did when she, with good intention, asked prayer for a member of the parish whose own children did not yet know she was hospitalized.

When deciding who knows what and when—and how—privacy and respect are the top priorities.

But I digress.

There are times, however, when the stories the pastor knows, the secrets confided to the pastor are less weighty than confession but far more consequential than general public knowledge. Pastors often know the truth about a situation whose consequences are dark. We know about the extramarital affair, the problem drinking, the troubled child, the untreated mental illness, the financial instability. The pastor often knows the painful truth of peoples' lives and holds those truths close to her heart.

The pastor is then sometimes caught in a bind when asked to comment on a situation, or when false information is being shared publicly. When I am tempted to correct the record or support the maligned or add to a conversation, I ask myself, "Is this my story to tell?"

Connie was a fourth-generation member of our congregation and our best volunteer. She quilted and baked and sang and taught and helped out in the church office.

Her parents and grandparents and great grandparents were long dead, but people spoke of them with great affection and respect. The building's foundation had been poured by her grandfather's construction company, and he had served as chair of the property committee for decades. Her father had served multiple terms as president of the Congregation Council and as chair of every call committee for ten pastors in a row. Her mother had taught Sunday school to three generations of children. The family had a reputation for generosity with their time, their expertise, and their wealth. People often told me, "I wish you could have met Connie's dad. He was the best. And she's just like him." We couldn't get through a congregational meeting without someone saying, "If Old Man Butler was here, you know what he would say," and everyone would chuckle.

Connie only smiled when people spoke nostalgically of her parents. I assumed it was the practiced stance of a child whose parents are famous. Smile and nod. Smile and nod.

But one morning as the quilters were packing their things away, Connie rapped lightly on my door. "Do you have a minute?" I always had a minute for Connie: "Sure. What's up!"

Her lower lip began to tremble, her eyes to well with tears. Her hands began to shake. I took her threatening-to-spill Styrofoam coffee cup away before she dropped it, and guided her to a chair.

"It's my dad," she said. "He wasn't the person everyone thought."

It turns out that Connie had been the Keeper of the Family Secret for decades, but now, as the congregation prepared to break ground for a new education wing, the Butler Building, she could keep the secret no longer.

"Have you ever wondered why none of my brothers and sisters go to church here?" she asked. "Did you ever notice that I say nothing when people talk about my folks? My father was a wicked man. My grandfather, too. Nobody knows what it was like to grow up with them."

She told of the beatings her father had inflicted on her mother. Once, when her mother threatened to leave, he locked her in the basement for a day to teach her a lesson. Connie remembered the threats he had made to the children if anyone outside the family ever knew.

Though her father had never physically harmed her or her brothers or sisters, they were subject to violent verbal tirades without provocation. Connie confessed to knowing that her father had a mistress her mother never knew about. She had reason to believe she had a half sibling in a nearby town. Her siblings had fled the scene as soon as they were able to do so, but Connie remained close to home for her mother's sake.

"Can you even imagine what it has been like to hear about my Amazing Dad all these years? Old Man Butler this and Old Man Butler that. Everyone at church loved my Dad. He walks on water here. But at home? Oh my God . . .

"I swore I would never tell anyone, but now that we're getting ready to build this building, it's all coming back. People keep asking if my brothers and sisters are coming for the groundbreaking. They say, 'You must be so proud.' I had to tell somebody."

Part of me was in disbelief. The man she described bore no resemblance to the saint of whom everyone spoke. But I knew that many congregations have a respected elder, a patriarch or matriarch, whose private failings put the lie to their public face. I also knew that Connie had nothing to gain by maligning her long-dead father. I believed her. And ached for her.

A hundred questions raced through my mind, but my concern at that moment had to be for Connie. Telling this story had taken every ounce of courage she had, and I needed to support her. "What can I do?" I asked. "How can I help?"

"I'd like you to tell everybody what a fake he was. I'd like you to call off the whole Butler Building nonsense. I'd like you to 'out' him." Long pause. "But that would be wrong and petty and vindictive. And nothing good would come of it. I guess I just need to know that you know."

Pastors are privileged to hear peoples' stories every day. Rarely are those stories so dark, so troubling as Connie's. I lay awake that night and many nights after, praying over a course of action. It would have served no good purpose to expose Connie's father, to sully his memory with the truth about his family life. The only person who would be harmed by such revelations would be Connie, and she had been harmed enough.

As the day for the groundbreaking drew nearer, as I heard more and more stories about what an amazing man Connie's father had been, my tongue was bloody (metaphorically speaking) for biting it. I knew a story I could not tell. I knew that we had to go ahead with our plans to honor the Butler family. I knew that Connie and her husband would attend the celebration, pretending to be glad.

I couldn't change the events of the groundbreaking or Connie's difficult childhood, but I could be of help to her in other ways. We found others to turn the first shovels of earth at the groundbreaking. I made plausible excuses for her brothers and sisters who chose to be absent. We included the names of other respected members, living and dead, in our prayers of thanks that day, not only the Butlers. And more than once, as earth was turned and prayers were prayed and champagne was poured and photos were snapped, I met Connie's eye.

As the festivities were breaking up, the shovels put away and the paper cups tossed in the garbage, Connie approached me silently. She touched my shoulder, whispered, "Thank you." Then she and her husband walked to their car, holding hands, grateful the day was over.

We each have a story to tell. Some we tell with great delight, the story growing grander with each telling. But some stories can never be told, are best hidden from public view. The pastor knows them all. But shouldn't those secrets, those stories, those confessions be safe with the pastor?

I knew Martha's story—that she was a proud, independent, and clear-minded woman. I knew that her children loved her deeply. I still wonder if I should have been more vocal in my support of them when the whole town turned against them. No harm would have ensued if I had said, "Martha and her family have been planning for this possibility for years. I'm proud of them and you should be, too."

I knew Connie's story—that she was the bearer of a terrible family secret. And though I was tempted to speak, to say something cryptic like, "Old Man Butler might not have been all we thought he was," it would have served no good purpose.

Martha and her children were glad that I knew, as was Connie. They didn't expect or need me to speak. It was enough that I knew.

Everybody has a story. They need to know that their secret is safe with me.

Your Secret Is Safe Questions for Discussion

1. What is the central dilemma posed by this essay?

2. How does a pastor discern the difference between information that ought to be confidential and what might be more broadly known?

3. To what extent might a congregation expect the pastor or church office to be the communication hub for information about other members of the congregation?

3

This Far, and No Farther

Whenever we go out to dinner, my husband affectionately teases me, "Who else will be joining us?" He knows me too well. I have befriended most of the waitstaff at our local Italian restaurant, and cannot get through a meal without asking about Rosemary's homebound mother, or Lauren's graduate school progress. Inevitably, we end up in conversation over dinner with someone interesting.

My daughters find my fascination with other peoples' lives amusing. They tease me by posing new and awkward interpersonal challenges. "Mom, ask the mechanic for his wife's middle name. I bet he'll tell you!"

People are hungry to talk about their lives, to tell you how they are if you really meant it when you asked, to share their stories with someone who will listen all the way to the end without jumping in with, "You know, that's like the time I—." The manager at Clark's Shoe Store and Dawn, the dental hygienist, and the docent at the historical society all have stories to tell, if only someone pays attention.

Paying attention. Asking people how they are and caring about the answer. Treating strangers like human beings. Spending a little extra time. Paying attention means there is no such thing as a quick trip to the grocery store, but does it really matter if the milk is a little warm when I get home?

Pastors are expected to do so many things well, it wears me out just thinking about it. Expectations real and unreasonable fill each day to overfull. But people will forgive the tedious sermon, the missed meeting, the pointless newsletter article, if they believe the pastor cares about their lives. At the risk of being hopelessly minimalistic, paying attention means more to the people in our care than any carefully managed agenda or pitch-perfect chant ever could.

Frank was an unlikely candidate for a heart attack. Fit and trim, disciplined and determined, he was the youngest sixty-year-old I have ever met. Recently retired from civil service, he and Carolyn were giddily planning a long retirement. For that reason, the midnight phone call was more shocking than such phone calls usually are. "Is this the pastor? A member of your parish is in our ER. Here, you can talk to his wife." Before Carolyn said good-bye, I was dressed and out the door. I think my car has a "cloaking device" that shields it from state troopers as I speed down highways late at night. In NASCAR-placing time, I rocketed to the hospital, slammed the car into park, and galloped into the emergency room.

Haunted by the ghosts of his father and grandfather and uncles, all felled by heart attacks, Frank struggled for life. Through that night and into the next day, physicians battled to stabilize Frank's condition. The crisis passed eventually and Frank started the slow climb toward strength. Sadly, Frank's precarious physical health was complicated by a deep depression that he could not shake. He later admitted that, knowing his family history, he was certain that when his heart first clutched in his chest that night, he was going to die.

I spent more time with Frank and Carolyn than with my own family those days. I was a frequent visitor, both at the hospital and later at the house, sometimes only stopping by to check-in and other times staying longer for communion and conversation. "Don't bother knocking," Carolyn said, "You're always welcome, day or night." Rufus, the dog, didn't even bark when I and other concerned friends and neighbors stepped into the house; he just sighed and returned to his dreamy rabbit hunt.

As Frank's strength improved and he tiptoed cautiously back into ordinary life, we knew our everyday/all-day contact had to end. Soon enough, it was time for them to pay attention to their lives, and for me to attend elsewhere. But we missed each other. We still do.

Not all medical emergencies demand or even expect such dogged pastoral attention. But in this circumstance, with this family, at this time in their lives, daily contact was completely appropriate. Paying attention to the needs of the parish means the pastor must be able to determine when a family needs attention and when it wants to be left alone—whether the pastor's presence is more valuable at the onset of the crisis or once it eases. Paying attention is not a one-size-fits-all pastoral technique. It is a skill honed by careful listening and clarity about the pastor's place in times of trauma.

One of my ongoing struggles as a pastor is to temper my inherent interest in peoples' lives with the understanding that not everyone understands the "rules." Most people in our parishes understand about the pastor's attention. They know that we care about them, and lots of other people, too. They realize that the pastor hears lots of stories, not only theirs. They know that no matter how intimate the conversation or how strong a bond of trust, at the end of the day the pastor returns to her own life and home. The pastor listens out of genuine interest and concern, but does not rely on those pastoral relationships for personal sustenance. Nor can the parish member expect that the pastor is devoted solely to their needs or concerns.

Unfortunately, every once in a while the pastor's attention is misunderstood. The parish member imagines a unique relationship with the pastor that can only, ultimately, disappoint.

A lonely man stays later and later on Sundays, believing that the After Worship Handshake is more than just a friendly greeting.

A troubled woman drives slowly by the church office every afternoon, stopping if the pastor's car is in the lot. "You said I could stop by anytime," she announces, plopping down in a chair.

The new widow doesn't understand why the pastor can't have afternoon coffee as often as she did in the first weeks after the funeral.

How do you tell the lonely man, the troubled woman, the recently widowed that their lives matter to you, but others' lives do, too? How do you break the news that that the pastor's time and touch and tears are shared with lots of people? And how often do we need to be reminded that the people in our parishes and in the grocery store have stories to tell that no one else wants to hear?

For me, this sort of misunderstanding happens even outside the walls of the church. I will never forget the embarrassment of admitting to the woman pouring her heart our over the red peppers in the grocery store produce section that I didn't know who she was. Apparently, in a dentist's waiting room, we had started a conversation about her mother's illness, and she was glad to see me, to bring me up-to-speed at the grocery store.

Pastoral Life

"Paying attention" seems a dying art—an art that I practice at my own pastoral peril.

Sometimes I sneak into my office on Saturday morning, hoping to get work done without the daily interruptions of phone calls and foot traffic. I park my car behind the building out of street-view, pull the window shades, keep the lights off and the doors locked, dreaming of undisturbed time to work. But I suspect there is a "pastor cam" somewhere that I can't see, alerting others to my presence in the office. Inevitably, within ten minutes of logging on to my computer and powering the coffeemaker, the phone rings or a car pulls up or someone is pounding on the church door.

Janet showed up at the church office on just such a Saturday morning. Most times, when someone pounds on the door on Saturday or after hours, I just let them pound. But I knew something was up when Janet's car appeared in the lot. She had been worshipping with us for a while, but I did not know her well. I could tell she carried a burden, that something troubled her, but she had not opened the door to conversation, so I had not knocked. Standing sheepishly at the church's front door that sunny Saturday, she told me it had taken all her courage to drive by the church that morning. She hoped I wouldn't be there so she would not have to tell her story. But there I was, and the coffee was on, so we sat down to talk.

Over the next two hours, Janet choked out a tearful story of childhood abuse and neglect. She had run away from home in her teens, had done things of which she was tremendously ashamed. She had spent her adult life trying to put those terrible years behind her, but she said lately she had been having troubling dreams, and decided she needed to talk. I sat in silence as she stumbled through her story of sorrow and shame. Exhausted, she just looked at me when she was done.

"Do you hate me?" she whispered.

"No, I don't hate you. But I am too sad to speak right now."

We sat silently for a time, finally breaking the silence with prayer, our words punctuated by fat tears plopping on her denim lap.

Janet was not in worship that week. Or the next. Or the next.

When we finally made contact, she confided that she had stayed away for fear that I was disgusted by her, that her confession had been repulsive to me. I assured her that she could not be more wrong, that it would be an honor to be her pastor. We agreed to meet again, but only if she also agreed

This Far, and No Farther

to see a therapist whom I trusted. Janet needed more than the friendly neighborhood pastor if she were to survive the work of recovery that lay before her.

Over the course of the next year, Janet joined our congregation, helped out with fall and spring work parties on the church grounds, volunteered as a reader with our preschool. Every time she was in the building, she stopped by to say "hey." She told me about her day, or thanked me for putting her in touch with the therapist, or asked how I was doing.

Gradually, her interest in me became more personal. The first sign of trouble was an invitation to stop by her house on a Saturday morning for a cup of coffee, "just the two of us." Her birthday gift to me was a little excessive. An exquisite bouquet of flowers delivered to my home, the card signed simply, "Thanks," caused my husband to raise a quizzical eyebrow.

I continued to tell myself she was simply being grateful, that pastoral attention was new to her and perhaps a little overwhelming. But something inside me knew that was not true. I shared my concerns with the church staff, all of whom warned me to be careful. They reminded me that people often become unduly attached to a pastor (especially to me), and that I needed to be very clear about boundaries with Janet.

Futilely, I speculated about her devotion to me. Was I a mother figure? The friend she never had? A latent love interest? Was she mentally unbalanced? Had she been a man, I would have been far more cautious. But, regardless of her intent or my growing apprehension, I continued on my merry way, naively imagining that Janet understood "the rules" of our relationship, that she meant no harm, that her interest in me was benign.

My naiveté was almost my undoing when one night, I was alone in the building after a late meeting. As I went to lock the church's front door and head for home, Janet appeared on the other side of the glass door. "Let me in?" she asked. She raised a bottle of wine in one hand and a corkscrew in the other. "I thought we'd share a glass of wine."

I was stunned. What in the world was Janet doing at the church door at that hour? What made her think it was okay to catch me alone? Had she already been drinking? What did she think was going to happen if I let her in? I knew no good would come of inviting her in, or having any conversation at all that night.

Wobbly with fear but resolved to be firm, I stepped back from my side of the door and shook my head. "No, we can't have a drink. I'm going home now. You need to leave."

"Just one glass?" she begged. "What could it hurt?"

"You need to leave now."

She suddenly turned tearfully belligerent. "I only wanted to talk. You're always so busy and I knew I could find you here. I waited for everybody else to leave."

"You need to leave now or I'm calling the police."

"I thought we had something special. I told you everything and you were so nice to me. But then you didn't have time for me anymore and there are always other people around and I just want to talk to you."

"You need to leave now, or I will call the police."

Slowly, never breaking eye contact, she backed into the darkness toward her car. I waited until her car drove away, then called my husband and asked him to come and walk me home. I didn't want to step into the darkness alone.

Paying attention. It can be a dangerous pastime.

My natural curiosity about people combined with pastoral access pulls me into all manner of quirky and profound conversations. But I imagine the same is true of most pastors. We delight in hearing about the high school basketball game or the Ladies Book Club selection or the hymn that touched a worshipper's heart. All we need to do is pay attention. Listen more than we speak. Ask and not anticipate the answer. Show concern and mean it.

Then, when sorrow strikes, or trouble falls out of the sky, or unanswerable questions get asked, the pastor who has been paying attention is naturally a part of the conversation.

A pastor can never know if pastoral attentiveness will be understood or misconstrued. Frank and Carolyn knew intuitively that their pastor's undivided attention was necessitated by crisis, and would not last. Janet, on the other hand, believed the pastor's attention was utterly unique, and she had a hard time accepting the limits of our relationship.

Foolishly, I assume others think about the world as I do. I assume good intentions on the part of others. I tend to give people the benefit of the doubt, and, in so doing, often unwittingly accommodate odd or even unacceptable behavior. Coupled with my generally chipper view of human nature is my deep fascination with peoples' lives. So dramatically for me, but probably for all pastors, attention must be paid to careful boundary setting in all parish relationships. The pastor must cultivate appropriate arenas for that innate curiosity and interest. He must nurture relationships with family and friends that make it possible for him to keep interested but at an appropriate distance from the lives of his parishioners.

As much as I love the people I serve, I cannot encourage their affection to satisfy my own needs. And they need to know that the pastor's attention is sincere, but limited. Taking God's admonition to Job wildly out of context, the pastor needs to say, "This far shall you come, and no farther." (Job 38:11)

When the phone rings, when the door knocker bangs, when help is needed, the pastor pays attention. She pays attention to the person in need, and close attention to that welcoming-but-real boundary between faithful care and dangerous obsession.

Pastoral Life

This Far, and No Farther Questions for Discussion

1. What is the central dilemma portrayed in this essay?

2. How might a pastor determine appropriate levels of attention in a particular circumstance? How is that determination communicated?

3. When is it appropriate for the pastor to deny or provide a limited response to a request for attention?

4. How could congregation members be encouraged to articulate their expectations to the pastor?

4

May I Come In?

"Tell Pastor not to visit. I don't want to see anyone. I don't want to talk to anyone. I want to be left alone." The instruction on the office voicemail was clear. Her children, her friends, her neighbors (but for one)—all of us were banished for the duration of her mending.

Marlene had suffered a fall in her home, coming away with bruised buttocks and wounded pride. Uncharacteristically agreeable, Marlene was obeying her doctor's orders to spend a week in bed. Her children had arranged the bedroom and bath so Marlene had everything nearby. A neighbor had permission to check on her twice a day, bringing fresh food and water. The telephone and TV remote were in easy reach. The mail was being collected and kept.

I didn't like her orders, but I understood. Never mild-mannered, Marlene was going to control her recovery as she controlled every other aspect of her life. She had lived alone for twenty years after her husband's death. She would not be a burden on anyone. She could take care of herself. Marlene was also embarrassed about the accident. A seventy-five-year-old woman ought not be bumping butt-first down the stairs with a laundry basket. Having suffered the indignity of EMT's and hospital gowns and allowing health professionals to boldly go where no man had gone in a long time, she was not about to be analyzed abed in her threadbare cotton bathrobe, her helmet-hard white hair a rat's nest, those brilliant red talons chipped. "I will not be an exhibit at the zoo, a fish in a bowl for everyone to look at and pity."

Trusting that her needs were met and her request real, I made a note in my calendar to wait a week before paying a pastoral call. I believed that Marlene really wanted to be alone.

How stupid of me. Initially, she might have enjoyed the idea of suffering in silence, gritting her teeth through the dark nights of pain and incapacitation, emerging at the end of the week ready to run the world again.

But after two days with none but Alex Trebek and Wolf Blitzer for company, Marlene was climbing the walls. Bored. Self-pitying. Desperately out-of-the-loop. She would never last a week without people. But she was stuck. Marlene had been militarily direct in her instruction to be left alone. How was she to get people back into her life and her home without appearing weak or helpless? I imagine she paced back and forth in her brain all night that second night, plotting her next move.

The first phone call was to her neighbor, asking for an extra visit that day—there was a funny noise coming from the refrigerator. The second call was to her best friend, just checking to find out if her azaleas were blooming yet. Word quickly spread that Marlene was receiving phone calls; telephones lit up all across town. Soon, the driveway was full of cars, the answering machine full of messages, the refrigerator (whose funny noise had stopped of its own accord) full of food. Of course, everyone but the pastor knew that Marlene had changed her mind about visits. I was the only one foolish enough to have believed her, though others had taken the bait initially, as well.

By the fourth day of her "confinement," the phone was ringing at the church office with odd questions about my whereabouts. "Is Pastor out-of-town? Is she home with a sick child?" It was not until I overheard one of the quilters whispering to her sewing partner, "Did you know Pastor doesn't visit the sick anymore?" that I realized I was the only one not in on the news that Marlene was back in control.

There are some who crave the company of the pastor. They can't imagine the pastor has anything else to do but visit them. Most days, this myopic vision of the pastor's work is amusing and quaint. They view the pastor as a dateless high school girl, sitting anxiously by the phone on Saturday night, willing it to ring. This attitude is already dying. However, there is nothing quaint or amusing about discovering that one of the flock is in need of pastoral care, and everyone knows but the pastor.

To compound the conundrum, imagine the confusion that occurred with Marlene:

a. The pastor knew about the need.

b. The pastor was instructed to stay away.

c. The pastor learned (too late) that B was a test.

Caring for the members of the parish is indeed part of the pastor's call, but not the only task, nor the primary one. Parish visitation is a task that can be scheduled, fit into other demands of the day. Emergencies change every plan but, for the most part, visiting the sick and homebound is folded into the rhythm of the pastor's work. In fact, it gives me great pleasure to sit at the kitchen table, in the nursing home sunroom, at the hospital bedside sharing conversation both mundane and profound. I often grieve the lack of time needed to simply "be" with people.

That said, I must also confess that my colleagues and I are often guilty of inattentiveness, of letting other matters shoulder out time that could be spent in homes and hospitals. There is no excuse for this lapse, though this failure is rarely born of wicked intention.

Marlene and I recovered from our misunderstanding. Her friends admitted that my absence was innocent. I check on Marlene regularly now, just to be on the safe side.

I am a big fan of PBS's *Masterpiece Theater*, especially the Jane Austen dramas. Sunday nights at my house are often spent in front of the television, decoding thick British accents and tea customs, admiring the blousy Victorian regalia, marveling at the rolling countryside, falling in love with Mr. Darcy, over and over again. One of the stock characters in these lovely, bucolic dramas is the country priest. He is a soft-bodied, limp-wristed, affected, and ineffective lamb of a fellow, solicitous of rich widows and unmarried farmers' daughters.

According to Ms. Austen, the country priest spent all his time writing simpering sermons disastrously delivered, and sipping tea. These fictional priests did not have to contend with writing unread reports, endless meetings, staff supervision, curriculum development, community organizing, budget management, intermittent internet connections, daily blogs, drop-in visitors, or any of the other interruptions that define the contemporary pastor's portfolio.

If there ever was a time or a place when the pastor/priest had nothing to do but travel house-to-house paying calls on the locals, I never lived in it. Of course, such an expectation of pastoral ministry also demands that someone be at home to be visited. More often than not, every house in the neighborhood is empty by eight thirty in the morning or, if someone is home, the day is tightly planned. Even some of our "homebound" are only homebound for church purposes—they manage trips to the casino and grandchildren's ballet recitals just fine. "Regular parish visiting," routinely included in the pastor's letter of call, depends on both the pastor's time and the parishioner's availability.

Visiting is a good thing. It is just not as simple as it would appear.

Having been a pastor longer than not, I often forget that the pastoral office and the person of the pastor can matter a great deal. "Visitation" is an important event for both pastor and parishioner. In fact, Visitation is the official title given the Angel Gabriel's unsolicited appearance to the unsuspecting Virgin Mary. One hopes that the visitation offered by pastors is less stealthy and startling than that modeled by Gabriel, but the impact of that encounter between mortal ministers and the possibly no-longer-virgin should not be discounted.

To many, the pastor is a trusted friend. The pastor's words bring comfort. The pastor's presence imbues a crisis with calm. The pastor carries God into the room. For a twisted few, a visit from the pastor is a game with points scored for number of visits, length of visit, and most information gleaned. But for most, especially the elderly and alone, the pastor is a warm, comforting presence in a cold, unpredictable world.

I have seen no studies on the subject, but I have the distinct impression that the church is increasingly populated by people who see little value in the pastor's visit or even the pastoral office. If the elderly expect the pastor to be a regular occupant of the kitchen chair, some of the younger cannot imagine such an event. It is a confusing time for pastors. Which is to be heeded—the voice that demands attention or the voice that dismisses it?

I have long had the practice of making telephone contact with worship visitors. That said, I don't usually call after a single visit. After all, one can never know if the visitor was there to worship, or simply staying warm while AAA fixed a flat tire in the church parking lot. But it is a pleasure for me to welcome visitors to the congregation, to tell them about our ministry, and to learn about theirs. In years past, these phone calls were met with genuine gratitude, and sometimes with real delight. Often, the initial phone call would result in an invitation to coffee at their home or an appointment at my office.

May I Come In?

But in recent years, these well-intentioned, cheerful phone calls have been greeted with stony silence. With few exceptions, most phone calls to a worship visitor now result in never seeing that person or family again. Even "welcome" postcards and notes have later been deemed a boundary violation. What I regard as hospitality is seen by some as irrelevant or even threatening. Was it something I said?

Kristie sneaked in the church doors on a brisk January day, as the last notes of the prelude reverberated through the room. I noticed her almost immediately, in large part because not many people under the age of sixty worshipped at that early hour. She was also conspicuous because she sat alone, clutching her winter coat like a shield around her, fidgeting, with one eye always on the exit. From my vantage point in the chancel, it was clear she wasn't a complete stranger to worship. The hymnal didn't frighten her. The complicated menu of options we call "communion distribution" didn't dissuade her. But before the organist's fingers lifted from the keyboard at the end of the postlude, she was out the door. Kristie gave our well-meaning volunteers the slip weeks in a row, affording them no opportunity to shake her hand or offer her a cup of coffee. I watched her diminutive, coat-clad figure slip quietly through the back door for a full month of Sundays before someone stopped her long enough to retrieve her name and phone number.

I made my customary "hey howdy" phone call; she agreed to a visit. But something was amiss. There was hesitancy in Kristie's voice that concerned me. On the morning of our visit, I fully expected a voicemail message cancelling the appointment with that ubiquitous excuse, "Something has come up." But there was no such cancellation, so at the appointed hour I appeared on her doorstep.

"Awkward" does not begin to describe our encounter. It was not clear Kristie was going to invite me in. Eventually, she ushered me to a straight-back chair just inside the front door. There was no offer of a cup of coffee or a glass of water. She stood a few feet away from me, arms crossed across her chest as I tried to launch a friendly conversation. Finally she blurted out, "What do you want? I haven't slept a wink since you called. I talked to people at the office today about this and they said I shouldn't tell you anything, or sign anything. I'm a good person with nothing to be ashamed of."

With help from the perfectly timed irruption of her ridiculously cute yellow Lab puppy, Barnabas, we recovered from that prickly start. I assured her that my intentions were benign, that I only wished to welcome her to our congregation. The visit was not long. She signed nothing (not that I asked her to). Kristie worshipped with us a few more times, but then disappeared as mysteriously as she had appeared. I did not pursue her.

I agonized over this bizarre meeting for weeks. Finally, I shared my confusion with another family new to the parish, one of the few I had called who didn't run screaming into the night. Steve and Marcy are the same age as Kristie. They are lifelong Christians, hardworking teachers, wonderful parents to their high school children. I respect and admire them enormously. I figured I could trust them with my confusion.

As I described Kristie's reaction to my visit, they smiled pastorally at me. Gently, they explained that, for many, the pastor is a service provider.

"You are like the dentist," they said. "Your dentist cleans teeth and fills cavities. Your dentist provides a clean, safe space for you. Your dentist might even see you on a Saturday in an emergency. The dentist is a wonderful person whose skills you admire. But that's all. No one invites the dentist to come for tea. No one wants the dentist in their kitchen or on the front porch. If your dentist appeared unannounced at your front door, you would have every right to call the police."

We sat in silence for a moment.

"So why did you let me visit when you were new to the parish?"

They regarded me with the patient bemusement one reserves for a doddering aunt. "We could tell you wanted to visit. We knew you needed to."

My head was spinning. Me? Pathetically needy? Me? Just another service provider?

Steve and Marcy have moved way past the "pastor pity" stage, and, on their advice, I am more nuanced about my approach to worship visitors. But their analysis of a world in which the pastor is "just another service provider" is a world I am still learning. It is a world as foreign as a *Masterpiece Theater* world, in which the pastor does nothing but drink tea with rich widows.

Thinking back to Gabriel's pouncing pastoral call on a first-century Mary, I wonder if the Angelic Visitor might have to alter his approach in the twenty-first. Maybe a request to be Facebook friends would precede that initial visit. Perhaps Gabriel's advance team could put a postcard in Mary's mailbox, announcing Gabriel's visit to her neighborhood in coming weeks. Or it might be that Mary would receive a phone call at supper time, "This is not a solicitation. Please don't hang up. We have an important offer for you." Text messaging "I want 2 C U" is an option. Could Gabriel make his case in 144 Twitter characters?

Regardless of the approach, swooping down on Mary as she slept would not be a good idea. In this century, the Visitation would then necessarily refer to the Heavenly Host who bailed Gabriel out of the county jail on charges of home invasion.

My pastoral colleagues differ on the best approach to staying in touch with members and friends of the parish. My retired pastor friends grieve the lost art of the Pastoral Call, remembering the years when home and hospital visitation was a primary pastoral task. My younger colleagues rely heavily on social media for communication within the parish, preferring Skype meetings to face-to-face ones.

I find myself in the Muddled Middle Generation. I love visiting in peoples' homes and work places, but find it increasingly difficult to do so. It is a real time-saver to communicate online, though it still feels a bit impersonal to me. There are some conversations that are best in person, and other times when a texted ☺ is all that is needed. I've prayed with people over the phone, though to me it is a bit like kissing through a screen door.

Sometimes we cannot be present with one another in the flesh. Sometimes physical presence is not desired. Time and distance, circumstance and expectation stand in the way of or preclude a face-to-face encounter.

All I know is this: only angels are allowed unannounced visits. The rest of us have to ask permission. May I come in?

May I Come In? Questions for Discussion

1. What is the central dilemma posed by this essay?

2. What is the purpose of pastoral visitation?

3. Which of these methods of contact between pastor and parishioner/visitor is most welcoming/least threatening to you?

    1. Facebook
    2. Telephone call
    3. Letter or card
    4. E-mail
    5. Text message
    6. Scheduled visit
    7. Unscheduled visit
    8. "Thanks for visiting" gift
    9. Something else _____

5

I Don't Know Your Life

Standing in a long line at a fast food joint, impatient with hunger and a short lunch hour, I fumed about the disagreement happening at the counter. A customer at the head of the line was talking on the phone, arguing with the attendant, adding to her order exponentially. Was she ordering for the whole U.S. Olympic Swim Team? The acned attendant behind the counter was clearly exasperated and, when the order was finally placed, asked sharply, "Here or to go?" The customer flew into a rage. "Do you really think I ordered all that food for myself?"

The tired teen sighed, "Lady, I don't know your life."

Where I'm from, that exchange would never have taken place. In a town as small as my hometown, everybody knew everybody's life. Or thought they did. The only unknown commodities were the occasional new school teacher, or the new Methodist pastor who moved in every seven years. We laugh at ourselves when we unthinkingly say, "Well, you know how the Smiths are." Once, when I was buying groceries for my parents at the small store on Main Street, the clerk studied me for a long time. "You're a Post kid, aren't you? You know, you all look the same."

But the illusion of "knowing" happens in communities large and small. When did the chubby-cheeked neighbor boy become that ridiculously handsome model on TV? Why did the much-loved high school football player take his own life? Who could have imagined the banker's wife would run off with the banker's best friend? We thought we knew them.

There is comfort in familiarity. We like to imagine that the people with whom we live and work are as easy to read as an open book, comfortable as an old shoe, reliable as a sunrise. But can any of us really fully know

Pastoral Life

another? And what changes in us when we see an unexpected aspect of someone we thought we knew?

A parish pastor is often confronted with conflicting information about a person whom we thought we knew. Sometimes we are surprised with a delightful revelation. When the quiet woman in the third pew reveals a flair for poetry, we delight to encourage her gift. But it is just as possible to be blindsided with harsh reality. I will never forget the day I opened the newspaper to a photograph of a seminary classmate, now a pastor. He was being interviewed about the recent discovery that a prominent member of his parish was, in fact, a serial killer. "We had no idea," he had muttered to the reporter.

Can we really fully know anyone? I often recall that befuddled fast food server who muttered, "I don't know your life." He spoke more truth than he knew.

Emile was quiet, seemingly always-old. She had never married, and had lived with her parents until they died. She was a doctor's receptionist for forty years—she knew everything about everyone, and yet said nothing. Emile was in church every Sunday, but never stayed for coffee or came to special events. "I enjoy my own company," she told me. The truth was that she was tremendously shy; standing around after church holding a weak cup of coffee was not her cup of tea.

As Emile aged, it became more and more difficult for her to get to church, but she adamantly refused a ride, so we added her to our homebound list. My first visit to her home confirmed what I had imagined about her. She lived in a small house on a quiet street in a modest neighborhood. Her furniture was nice and clean, but a bit worn. She poured tea from a beautiful china teapot with a chipped spout. Embarrassed about the flaw she said, "I remember my mother pouring from this pot. It's old, but I just can't let it go."

Though our congregation was enduring some financial difficulties, and we had discreetly asked some of our wealthier members to give a little more than usual, it never occurred to me to ask Emile. I assumed she lived on a modest retirement income, that her weekly gift to the church was little more than a widow's mite. Around the office we called her "Poor Emile."

Once when I visited, Emile was in a tizzy. Torn envelopes were scattered across the kitchen counter, their contents spilling on the floor. "Oh,

I Don't Know Your Life

Pastor," she sighed. "My nephew usually opens the mail and pays the bills, but he's working out of town and won't be here for another week. All this mail came at once. Can you help me sort it? I feel so helpless. I want everything to be ready for him."

Shrugging my coat onto her floral sofa and throwing my scarf over a kitchen chair, I gathered up a pile of papers to start sorting. It struck me as odd—this anxiety, this lack of organization was not like her at all. Later, I realized this odd behavior was a sign of early dementia, but at the moment I was confused by her confusion.

I was even more befuddled when I paid attention to what I was sorting. I assumed she was worried about sorting a pile of unpaid bills and advertising circulars. Instead, Emile had handed me a sheaf of financial documents—bank statements, quarterly investment reports, stock updates. According to the documents I held, she had hundreds of thousands of dollars in investments and savings. Who could have known that shy, modest Emile was loaded?

I had often worried that her finances were uncomfortably tight, so it was a relief to know she was not impoverished. But I have to admit that, seeing the size of her portfolio, my thoughts about "Poor Emile" suddenly shifted. "Maybe we could ask Emile to give a little more money to the church," I thought. I immediately slapped myself out of it. I didn't want to treat Emile any differently now than I had before I knew of her wealth. But the thought did cross my mind . . .

Pastors are as susceptible to assumed familiarity as anyone. We often joke with one another that every congregation is populated by the same cast of characters. The Elder Statesman. The Angry Loudmouth. The Never-married Church Mouse. The Perennial Council Member. The Full-Octave Warbler. The Persistent Troublemaker. The Wise Matriarch. All that differs from parish to parish is each character's name.

But pastors do a disservice to the people in our care when we lapse into the unthinking, "I know you." It is critical that we remain open to surprise, to the fact that the people in our pews are complicated and nuanced. We do further disservice when we treat a person differently when our biases and impressions are challenged. It's one thing to throw your arms around someone in delight, "You amaze me!" It's another to shun the person who is revealed to be more of a sinner than makes us comfortable.

Pastoral Life

For good or for ill, the pastor must guard against quick judgments or hasty assumptions. None of us can know the life or heart or mind or motives of another.

Warren didn't get to church very often after his wife died, and that was fine with him. She had loved church and church people and church suppers, and for forty-five years he had humored her by tagging along. But once the every-weekend pressure to perform was relieved, he stayed in his slippers and read the newspaper most Sundays. He might not have been much for church attendance, but he loved pastors. Because Warren hadn't traveled outside the state except during the war, the pastors, who usually hailed from somewhere far away, were a window into a larger world for him. "Tell me where you're from," he'd ask. "What did your father do for a living?" "What do you think about ____?" The pastor was plied with coffee, peppered with questions, told not to stay away too long. "I have more questions for you next time," he'd shout as the pastor closed the car door.

Warren reminded me of other Old Guys I'd known. He was a retired union welder, a proud veteran of World War II. He drove American cars, drank Kentucky bourbon, and cheered for the Packers. He was not a complicated guy. I thought I knew him.

One day, I asked him to tell me again how he and his wife, Bertie, had met. It was a story he loved to tell, and I never tired of hearing it. But this time, he added a surprise ending. "You know," he said, leaning conspiratorially across the kitchen table, "Bertie would never let me do more than kiss her on the cheek when we were dating. She said she wasn't going to let me get close to her until we were good and married." He leaned back and took another sip of coffee. "She might have waited for me, but I didn't wait for her."

He went on to tell me that he and his buddies would visit "those French women" during the war. He remembered standing in line, waiting his turn for a few minutes of comfort before heading back to camp. "For a couple of bucks, it was a lot of fun," he grinned. "It sure passed the time."

As Warren reminisced about his youthful escapades, I felt my body tighten, my bemused smile froze. Was this nice old man really boasting about visiting prostitutes? Or maybe this was confession. I was waiting for the "Can you believe I did that?" or "What was I thinking?" But there was no apology, no remorse. He smiled to himself as he spoke, never noticing

I Don't Know Your Life

my silence. His musing ended when he said, "But Bertie never knew. She didn't need to. She always thought she was the only one."

What I know of the realities and exigencies of war wouldn't fill a tea cup. I won't begin to parse the rightness or wrongness, the necessities or excesses of behavior in a war zone. What bothered me was the cavalier way in which Warren dismissed the secret he had kept from his wife. I had known Bertie only in her later years, but to her dying day she loved to tell the story of how they met, that she held him at bay until their wedding night. Bertie once said, with a wink at her husband, "Warren is such a good husband. Do you know anybody else who would have put up with that? But it was worth it, wasn't it?" And then she blushed.

I thought I knew him. I thought he was a nice old man, a good husband and father, a funny storyteller. And he was all that. But he was also a man who had lied to his wife about something that she had cherished; he had allowed her to believe that they had "kept" themselves for each other. And now, widowed and old, he was proud of that deceit. I still don't know what to do with that.

What is the pastor to do when she comes to know a member of the congregation too well? How does the pastor's impression of a person change when a new piece gets added to a person's puzzle? And why would a pastor be surprised at new information at all? Isn't everyone complicated? I'm not talking about the horrible discovery that a member of the congregation has committed a crime, or hides a second family. I'm talking about the ordinary surprises and disappointments that emerge in any relationship as it grows. It's only logical to accept that those discoveries would influence the pastor-parishioner relationship.

I know I am not alone in this struggle. In Sonnet 116, William Shakespeare cautions against such changeability when he writes, "Love is not love which alters when it alteration finds." Clearly, he had been tempted to alter his opinion a time or two.

But more valuable to me than consulting the Bard is to turn to Lutheran pastor and martyr Dietrich Bonhoeffer and his slim volume *Life Together*. Of the danger of altering one's view of another, Bonhoeffer writes:

> Because Christ stands between me and others, I dare not desire direct fellowship with them. As only Christ can speak to me in such a way that I can be saved, so others, too, can be saved only

> by Christ himself. . . . I must meet him only as the person he is in Christ's eyes. Human love constructs its own image of the other person, of what he is and what he should become. Spiritual love recognizes the true image of the other person which he has received from Jesus Christ.[1]

Bonhoeffer describes a relationship always mediated by Christ. Anytime, whether as a pastor or spouse, parent or friend, I burden another with my vision of who they ought to be, I get in the way of the relationship Jesus Christ desires for us. We treat one another most faithfully, in the most Christ-like fashion, when we see the other as Christ sees that one. And because I know that Christ views all created beings through the eyes of love and forgiveness, it is this vision of the other that the pastor must seek.

This means that rather than seeing Emile as a Financial Faucet for our congregation's needs or Warren as a Diabolical Deceiver, I see them as does Christ. Rather than objects to be used or judged by me, they remain brothers and sisters in Christ, flawed but forgiven, sinful but saved, loved not for any practical worth, but because they are loved by God.

Here is an example of how seeing the other only through Christ plays out in real life. I often preside at funerals for strangers. I often hear, "It must be hard to bury someone you've never met." Surprisingly, it is easier to bury a stranger than someone I have known forever. When presiding at the funeral of someone familiar, my thoughts and motives are too easily clouded by what I know of that person. The scoundrel taxes my ability to say something kind, while the saint goes into the ground in a shower of superlatives. Neither approach is helpful at the time of death. What I think or feel about the deceased has no bearing on the message I am called to preach. I am far more able to speak a gospel word of the stranger, because I know him only in and through Christ. There is no pretense of "knowing." My words and thoughts are uncluttered by previous experience. I am able to speak of Christ's power to seek and to save, to love and forgive without stumbling over my own experience of the person in the casket.

To know someone only in and through Christ is what we are called to do—in life and in death.

Over three decades of parish ministry, I have often been surprised or disappointed by people in my care. I have, no doubt, provided similar surprise or disappointment to them. The longer we love one another, the more apparent both our virtues and vices become. That is why it is critical

---

1. Bonhoeffer, *Life Together*, 35–36.

to adopt the mind of Christ, and to immerse myself in Bonhoeffer's soul-searing words.

No one is either seamlessly kind or terminally wicked. It should not matter if the person in our care is rich or poor, a convicted felon or on the Pope's short list for canonization. As pastor of a congregation filled with a wild variety of saint and sinner, my task is to see Christ in all whom I meet. Nothing more and nothing less.

I don't know your life. I can't. What a gift that not-knowing is. What matters is that I know you through Christ, who loved you enough to die for you. That is the only You I need to know.

Pastoral Life

I Don't Know Your Life Questions for Discussion

1. What is the central dilemma portrayed in this essay?

2. Describe a time when you delighted to learn something about another, or were blindsided with information you did not expect. Did it change your relationship to that person?

3. To what extent is your ability to see the other as Christ sees them affected by familiarity or unfamiliarity?

4. How might we learn to love the other as Bonhoeffer describes, only in and through Christ?

6

Time to Go

"How long will you stay?" It was the very first question they asked me. I was in the final stages of a parish call process, interviewing with a congregation for which I would be the sixth pastor in ten years. The rapid succession of pastors was the result of misbehavior, miscalculation and mistakes on everyone's part, though the previous pastors were eager to blame the congregation, and the congregation was more than happy to blame the pastors. The reasons for the revolving pastoral door are irrelevant, but the whiplash caused by the quick turnarounds had left the congregation wounded, disappointed, disillusioned and suspicious.

"How long will you stay?" It was asked by a recent widow, an elderly woman who had been very close to the previous pastor. He was a kind man who had tended her and her family during her husband's sudden illness and death. Not everyone was sad to see him go, but she was. For her, calling a pastor was like falling in love—it's a matter of giving your heart away, trusting it will not be broken. She did not want to be hurt again.

I had no way to know the specific concern behind her question, but my answer did not depend on particulars. My reply was probably more amusing to me than to this too-often-jilted congregation, and might have seemed a bit flip, but it was the most honest answer I could give.

"I could be dead by morning, or I could retire from here—somewhere between the two. That's how long I will stay."

It might seem odd to ask about the ending at the beginning. But we pay so much attention to the call process, to the courting and wooing, that little attention is paid to the end of a call. How does a pastor know when it is time to go? And when it is time to go, will the pastor leave well?

Pastoral Life

He was a tall, trim, model-handsome man who seemed to be everywhere at once. He was also unmarried, which meant that he was always available and always alluring. My Roman Catholic friends would call such a priest "Father Whatawaste," but he was "Hey Pastor Tom" to everyone from grade school children to police officers. Even people who didn't go to church regarded Pastor Tom as their pastor, the go-to guy for funerals and weddings and private baptisms. He kicked off every Memorial Day parade and firefighters' breakfast and Little League tournament. Under his leadership, the congregation grew like wildfire. They added to the building, brought on new staff, launched program after program to serve the throngs that followed him. They were like children dancing behind the Pied Piper.

It was hard not to like Pastor Tom, unless you knew him well.

I have only heard stories from community and parish members, since I was not around during Pastor Tom's ministry. This is what I know, so what I share with you is all secondhand information, often-corroborated, but not an eyewitness account.

Pastor Tom's public face was welcoming and cheerful, understanding and caring. But in private he was a tyrant. It was his way or no way. For example, when the finance committee chair raised questions about the budget shortfalls created by Pastor Tom's "generosity," he was quickly relieved of his chair. When a Sunday school teacher quietly asked why he had missed the previous night's teachers meeting, which he had promised to attend, he blew up at her. "I have more important things to do!"

Within a few years of arriving at the parish, Pastor Tom had assembled around himself a tight team of lay leaders and staff who obeyed him like zombie soldiers. Elections became pointless, since the same handful of people was elected each year. The parish secretary guarded him like a pit bull, keeping unpleasantness and questions far from his door. Staff members answered only to him, refusing to consider any idea but Pastor Tom's.

Not everyone was enamored with Pastor Tom, however, and eventually his genial nature wore thin. Stories began to pop up about Pastor Tom's quick temper. The lack of accountability on his part and the part of his staff raised eyebrows. "How does the director of music spend his time? Why did those four kids come home from retreat early? What happened to the money we received when Mrs. Womble died?"

Time to Go

    Suddenly, and without notice, Pastor Tom submitted his resignation from the parish. Most were shocked. Those who had suffered silently under his regime were relieved.

    On his last Sunday, after blackmailing the parish treasurer into a large, unauthorized "unused vacation" check, Pastor Tom stood beaming before the scores of people who had come to see him off. "Friends, it's been fun. But I've been called to a better congregation. A bigger congregation. A congregation that appreciates the gifts I bring. They want me to take them where you could never go. Wish me well!"

    Some wept. Jaws dropped. Quizzical glances were exchanged. A man who was there that day later told me, "I've never met such a manipulative self-promoter in my life. But people loved him. Go figure."

    It was bad enough that Pastor Tom had used the congregation for his own purposes, and that so many good and kind people fell for his slick shtick. Worse yet was that when Pastor Tom left, he didn't really leave.

    Many in the congregation, including his loyal staff and leadership cadre, kept Pastor Tom clandestinely up-to-date on what was happening. The new pastor, his successor, received nasty notes from Pastor Tom, offering unsolicited advice and criticism. Pastor Tom wrote letters to members, poisoning them against "that new guy." Pastor Tom snuck into town for private social events to which only his loyal fan base was invited. Unbeknownst to the "new guy," he visited homebound and hospitalized members, keeping them under his thrall.

    Pastor Tom was a god to some, the devil incarnate to others. (The same can probably be said of most pastors.) But his continued contact with the parish was unethical, self-serving, and destructive. I was not his immediate successor—another poor soul suffered that fate. But even when I arrived, years after Pastor Tom's departure, his ghost lingered.

    In a well-intentioned but misguided attempt to honor Pastor Tom's work, and at the request of the family, I invited him to offer a eulogy at the funeral of a longtime member of the parish. Instead of a eulogy, he delivered a thirty-minute self-congratulatory review of all the ways he had been important to the deceased, and all the amazing things he had done as pastor of the parish.

    His "fans" swooned with delight. Those who had been wounded and abused by him ground their teeth. I never invited him back.

Pastoral Life

Although Pastor Tom's story may not demonstrate it, most pastors and congregations develop a "feel" for the end of a particular ministry. It might be that the pastor and parish have accomplished their goals and each is ready for a new challenge. Perhaps the pastor receives an invitation to consider another call, and is drawn to that new ministry. It might be that the pastor has become too comfortable, has developed an "old shoe" quality and, though dearly loved, no longer provides the leadership the congregation craves. Some congregations can only stand to have a pastor around for a few years; they have a track record of short pastorates and woe to the pastor who tests their limits. Pastors also leave when they retire from a particular ministry and from parish ministry in general. On some occasions, a pastor leaves a call abruptly due to illness, accident or family trouble. On rarer occasions, a pastor is removed for misconduct or malfeasance. Regardless of the particular circumstance, most of us try to exit gracefully, leaving as little damage in our wake as possible.

To be sure, choosing to leave is not an issue in denominations in which pastors and priests are methodically moved by the diocese or district. In some cases, the bishop or the district superintendent says it's time to go. It is still important to leave well, to behave honorably upon leaving, but under such circumstances the reason for the pastor's departure is unquestioned and irrelevant.

Leaving well is a gift to the congregation, to the pastor, and to the pastor's successor. It is far healthier for a congregation to celebrate the end of strong ministry, than to resent the pastor who lingered too long. And it is a great gift to the congregation's new pastor to be welcomed with open arms, her arrival undimmed by the glow of the Late Great Pastor X or clouded by the shadow of the Pastor Who Wouldn't Leave.

I have stepped into both situations: following the pastor who left well and the pastor who just couldn't leave it alone. Trust me, the former is far preferable to the latter.

But how do you know? Is five years too short a pastorate? Twenty-five years too long?

There is no magic formula. A retired bishop of my acquaintance had the "8-9-10 Rule" for his pastors. At eight years of service, the pastor was to start thinking about a new call. At nine years, the pastor actively sought a new call. And at ten years, new call or not, the pastor left. The bishop believed that pastors, like fish, start to smell if left lying around too long.

Time to Go

But even that is not a fail-safe guideline. I know ministries that have been vibrant for decades, as the congregation and pastor work together to stay lively, healthy, and fresh. I have also seen congregations, especially rural parishes, that routinely call seminary graduates, teaching them how to be a pastor in a safe, welcoming environment and then, after just a few years, sending them off to another parish wiser, stronger, and ready for their new call.

How do you know when it is time to leave?

If the parishes I have served are to be believed, in each case they were sad to see me go. As was I. In fact, I left each call a little earlier than I might have otherwise because of changes in my husband's career. After all, we tease him, there is only so much demand for white guys with PhDs in systematic theology. Parish pastors, on the other hand, are a dime a dozen; I can find work anywhere. "Have collar, will travel," as they say.

When a pastor is called to a congregation, that congregation becomes the pastor's primary ministry focus. The pastor pours heart and soul into that ministry, not for her own sake, but the sake of the congregation and its witness to the gospel. The pastor weeps for sorrow, delights in good news, nurtures leadership, lies awake nights pondering and planning the challenges before the congregation. But when the call to that parish is ended, so, too, is the pastor's responsibility to that parish. The next pastor will take up the weeping and delighting, the nurturing and pondering and planning.

Another tricky move is for a pastor to maintain the handful of friendships she will carry with her, but to otherwise cut all pastoral ties to the parish. It is wrenching when someone from a previous parish asks the former pastor to be in touch with a member who is hurting, or to do a wedding or funeral for a former member. As much as the pastor longs to be helpful, those tasks belong to the pastor under call. It is then that the pastor must set aside personal feelings and ego and say, "I'm sorry, but I can't. I'm sure your pastor will take good care of you."

To leave well means the pastor is clear about the limits of the pastoral call, and her responsibility to the pastor who follows. After all, the pastor can be pastor of only one congregation at a time, and it is incumbent on the pastor to devote all her attention to the new call, thus assuring her successor is respected and honored.

As we ask the congregation in my denomination's rite of installation for pastors, "Will you pray for and honor your new pastor *for his/her work's sake*?" (italics mine) In other words, the congregation prays for and honors

49

the pastor because he is the pastor, regardless of personality or appeal or expertise. The former pastor can go a long way toward making that promise real—by staying out of the way, by leaving well.

Congregations help a pastor leave well when they recognize all that the pastor has brought to the ministry and celebrate it, burying any disappointments or criticism. The outgoing pastor does not need to be punished for inadequacies as she walks out the door. Nor does the new pastor need to hear about the excellence or the faults of the previous pastor. We carry forward all that is good and strong, having learned from failure and disappointment.

Parish ministry is not a beauty pageant or a popularity contest. Parish ministry is shared work for a specified period of time. And when it is done, it is time to go.

At 103, Ethel was the oldest member of the congregation. She was also the deeply respected widow of a previous pastor. Upon his death and her retirement, she had moved back to the community. Though she knew absolutely everyone in town, and had great gifts for ministry, she never interfered in the work of her husband's successors. Once, when I thanked her for her respectful support she said, "You can have it. I'm glad it's somebody else's to worry about."

I visited her often and we enjoyed each other's company. She also had a deep and abiding friendship with my predecessor, Pastor Davidson. They had been through much together. He had presided at her husband's funeral. He had welcomed her back into the community and congregation when she retired. He had consulted her when perplexed about the parish, all the while respecting her desire to be just another member of the congregation. In this, and a hundred other ways, he was a "pastor's pastor," the pastor we all want to be.

Pastor Davidson was also very good to me. Upon leaving that parish he was still within easy driving distance, but he never interfered in my work or the parish's process. I knew he maintained friendships with a few families in the parish, but their friendship was not publicized, and those friends were also deeply supportive of me. When he and I encountered each other at events and conferences, we met as trusted colleagues rather than fierce rivals.

Time to Go

When it was evident that Ethel's life was drawing to a close, the family and I were in daily contact. Her son, himself elderly, mused, "You don't get this old by giving up easily." More than once I was called to her bedside because time was short. And each time, she rallied to live a few more days. I knew Pastor Davidson cared for her deeply, so I contacted him as her condition deteriorated. "If you would like to see her," I said, "we would all welcome it." But he respectfully demurred. "She is in good hands with you. Give her and the family my love."

Ethel's last words were the Lord's Prayer, which she whispered with me and a nursing home staff member. She died that night as she had lived, without fanfare or fuss.

There was little to be done, since her funeral plans had been made decades before. I met with her children and grandchildren to discuss details. And I called Pastor Davidson.

Though the family had not asked, I knew that he would be a welcome guest at the funeral. I craved his kind, solid presence at my side as we laid this *Grande dame* of the faith to rest. He hesitated when I asked him to share presiding responsibilities—"It's not my place"—but finally agreed. "Only if I'm not in your way," he cautioned. He couldn't be in the way.

Ethel's funeral was like her, a model of hopeful restraint. This was no forced "celebration of life" but honest acknowledgement of death, sure promises of new life in Christ, and gratitude for a life faithfully lived. Pastor Davidson and I shared the load that day, his confident presence a gift to me and all who worshiped with us.

I once worried out loud with a congregational president about what my departure would do to the congregation's ministry—we were in the middle of a number of projects and I hated to leave them unfinished. "Pastor," he said, "tonight when you go home, fill the kitchen sink with water. Push your hand all the way to the bottom of the sink and then pull it out. Do you see what happens? Do you see the hole that's left? It's like you were never there. We'll be fine." And though this "life lesson" stung a bit, I knew he meant it kindly, and that he was right.

Sadly, it had been Pastor Davidson's unpleasant task to pick up the pieces after Pastor Tom. It was Pastor Davidson who received the scathing letters, who endured the disdain of Pastor Tom Loyalists, who suffered years of overhearing, "Well, he's not Pastor Tom." Why he didn't run screaming into the night, I will never know. But he endured with that congregation. He rebuilt its leadership core and its sense of purpose. Most important, he nurtured in them the belief that the ministry belonged to all of them, not only to the pastor and a chosen few.

When I took the call to that parish, I received a congregation with a strong desire to engage in ministry together and a deep respect for the pastoral office, rather than for a particular pastor. Pastor Davidson left that congregation well, enabling me to begin well, too. I am forever in his debt.

When a pastor is called to a congregation, she jumps in with both feet and her whole heart, fully engaged in the ministry of that congregation in that time and place. And when she leaves the congregation, whatever the circumstances of her departure, she steps completely away, trusting the ministry to the people and pastor who will follow.

As my mother says about us adult children when we descend noisily on the family home at the holidays, "It's good to see you come. It's good to see you go."

Pastor, it might be time to go.

Time to Go Questions for Discussion

1. What is the central dilemma posed by this essay?

2. Is the decision to end a parish call solely the pastor's, or might the congregation be involved, as well?

3. What is the value of "negotiating" the end of a call, as congregations and pastors do the beginning of a call?

4. How does a congregation help the pastor leave well?

Congregational Life

7

Can You Hear Me Now?

There was only one hiccup in my husband's dreams of pursuing a graduate degree in theology. Money. Graduate school costs money, and it was in short supply at that time in our lives—we were parish pastors with a small child and young-family bills. Our ability to tackle graduate school tuition on my single salary would require hefty scholarships or a winning lottery ticket. Much to our relief, Jim was invited to interview for a highly competitive, solve-all-our-problems graduate school scholarship. An academic familiar with the scholarship program cautioned, "Yeah, it's nice that you were granted an interview, but don't get your hopes up. Competition for that money is stratospheric. You won't get it. Nobody in theology does."

Jim flew off to interview and I stayed behind with our toddler, counting eggs that hadn't even been laid yet. I watched the clock in my office as Jim interviewed, worrying him through the conversation, four time zones away. I knew that immediately after the interview he would be racing to the airport and might not have time to call. Besides, he wouldn't know anything that day. I tried not to fret. As if. Finally, my phone rang. It was Jim, calling from the airport.

"I got it! I got the scholarship!" he shouted into the phone.

Tears filled my eyes. "Oh, Jim, I'm sorry. We'll figure out some way to pay for school."

Silence.

"JoAnn. Listen to me. I got the scholarship. School is all paid for and a stipend, too. We'll be fine. But I have to run, the plane is boarding. Love you."

I guess we hear what we expect to hear, regardless of what is actually said.

As a pastor and preacher whose most important tool is words, I sometimes wonder which task is harder—speaking the words or hearing them. There are times when both are a struggle, when, in spite of our best efforts, neither the speaking nor the hearing goes as planned.

The careful, thoughtful preacher spends time with a scripture text, reading it over and over, discussing it with colleagues and friends, getting inside the text's world before dragging the text into our own. Then, only after careful study and a week of pondering and prayer, do words appear on paper. I work very hard to let the text speak to me and through me, rather than using the biblical words as confirmation of something I would have said anyway, regardless of the text. The word of God shapes the preacher before the preacher shapes the words.

Every preacher I know has had the experience of stepping into the pulpit armed with the sermon that will change the world—his best work—only to watch it fall lifeless to the floor, twitching as it bores itself to death. In the same way, the sermon that I shudder to preach, a homiletical humiliation, is hailed as life-changing and heartbreaking. The only way to explain the chasm between the preacher's sense of the sermon and the ears on which it falls, is to blame it on the Spirit, the Spirit that makes more of us and our words than we ever could.

I have to confess: I have a secret weapon in the sermon-writing department. I was trained as a print journalist, forced to tell a story under deadline. Find the point. Make the point. Illustrate the point. Print. Because of that training, I am a lightning-fast writer, a verbal gun slinger. Bang! Bang! It's a sermon!

But I have pastor friends for whom writing is a painfully slow process, for whom each word is a tussle. They spend countless hours in sermon preparation, and are forced to orchestrate the whole work week so that Saturday night doesn't find them sweaty and sleepless.

There is no magic formula for preparing a sermon. Regardless of the method of preparation, whether sermon writing is pleasure or torture, it must be done. Because, even though our congregations may hear only what they want to hear, they deserve to hear something.

Can You Hear Me Now?

It was the Second Sunday of Easter; the gospel reading was from the Gospel of John in which Jesus first appeared to his disciples after the resurrection (John 20:19–31). Some congregations call it "St. Thomas the Associate Sunday," since senior pastors across the country are nursing mimosas and the *New York Times* that morning after a long Holy Week and Easter.

Sermons on this text usually skewer poor Thomas, completely missing the really intriguing matter of Jesus' Easter gifts to his disciples. Two gifts actually. First, he spoke peace to them—this from a man who only days before had known no peace, who had endured the torments of betrayal and capital punishment. Second, he breathed the Spirit into their ears, expecting that the Spirit's presence would send them into the world forgiving.

Peace. Forgiveness. Those are Easter gifts Peter Cottontail simply can't deliver.

The text was particularly poignant that Easter season. Our community had suffered an Easter evening murder-suicide. For reasons never clear, a grade school teacher was murdered by her garage mechanic boyfriend, who then turned the gun on himself. Parents spent the week assuring their school-age children that they were safe, that what had happened to their beloved teacher could not happen to them. Neighbors of the couple were left speechless—there had been no indication of trouble or tension between these young lovers. The parish priest with whom they had been planning a fall wedding sobbed through the funeral mass. We all knew either the victims or their families. There was no getting away from the devastating sorrow of their unexplainable deaths.

Seven days after the tragedy, I stepped into the pulpit, clutching Jesus' twin resurrection gifts in one hand and our community's grief in the other. I unfolded the word with care, parsing what it meant that the resurrected-but-still-wounded Jesus offered peace. I underscored the point that Jesus expected his disciples to practice forgiveness and to understand the dire ramifications of choosing not to do so. I promised that these first Easter gifts had been given to us, too: peace and forgiveness, gifts we desperately needed but could not manufacture for ourselves. I prayed my words brought comfort and hope.

Among our worshippers was a man I did not recognize, a visitor who had listened attentively, often taking notes as I preached. When it was his turn to shake my hand at the door after worship, he clasped it firmly in both of his. "Thank you, Pastor. It's been a long time since I've heard a pastor speak so forcefully in support of the death penalty."

I stared dumbfounded at his retreating figure. I know people don't always hear what I intended, but he heard something I didn't even say. I guess we hear what we want to hear.

I suffer a chronic case of Preacher's Disease. The symptoms of the syndrome include manic swings between the conviction that every word I utter is precious, and the deep fear that I drone dreck. I alternately find myself fascinating and foolish. The most dangerous side effect of the disease is that we come to think the preaching is all about us and our ability or failure to entertain or enlighten, coerce or convince.

It is easy to forget the central purpose of the sermon: the centuries-old invitation into the mysteries of God. Sadly, we have gone astray of that central, simple purpose. Some view the sermon as a chucklogue, simple amusement for tittering fans. Those who attended the Lake Woebegone School of Preaching believe preaching is merely the clever stringing of stories. Others imagine themselves Parson Parsing, lecturing on the minutiae of the original languages as though salvation depends on proper noun declension. For some, the sermon is an opportunity to dispense unsolicited advice, or teach a history lesson. And some of us have simply thrown in the towel, week after week testing the Spirit's patience by showing up unprepared, uninterested and uninteresting. I marvel that anyone shows up for worship at all—including the preacher—since too often the word we offer is simply not worth waking up for.

I take the Apostle Paul very seriously when he writes, "But how are they to call on one in whom they have not believed? And how are they to believe in one of whom they have never heard? And how are they to hear without someone to proclaim him?" (Rom 10:14).

What we do in the pulpit matters. And while a particular sermon might not win any awards, each one must be lovingly, rigorously, faithfully prepared and offered. There is no escaping the hard work that faces the preacher week after week.

That said, I also know that I place far too much responsibility for the preaching task on my side of the pulpit.

Paul writes, "I solemnly urge you: proclaim the message; be persistent whether the time is favorable or unfavorable; convince, rebuke, and encourage, with the utmost patience in teaching. For the time is coming when people will not put up with sound doctrine, but having itching ears, they will accumulate for themselves teachers to suit their own desires, and will turn away from listening to the truth and wander away to myths" (2 Tim 4:2–4).

For preaching to "work," both preacher and hearer must be prepared for and open to the Spirit's movement. The faithful few who dot our pews each week also bear responsibility for the preaching. Whether their ears itch or their thumbs twiddle, the hearer who comes to worship unprepared will receive exactly what she brings to the preaching task: nothing. It is not enough to simply put your butt in a pew, mumble through the hymns and liturgy, tolerate the sermon and gulp the meal. Those who get the most out of a sermon pray for the preacher, asking God to guide and inspire. Faithful hearers prepare themselves to hear, reading (perhaps even studying) the texts before arriving for worship. And whatever we might feel about the preacher personally, whether undue admiration or utter disdain, we leave our character assessments in the parking lot. Preaching is a team sport in which all take part, not an individual event to be judged. That is why I won't tack a pious "Amen" on the end of a sermon. Who am I to say when the word's work is done? Though the preacher may have stopped speaking, the Spirit has not necessarily stopped stirring. When preacher and congregation share the preaching, it is a conversation rather than a performance, an invitation rather than a pronouncement. The preacher doesn't get to choose the ending, only the trajectory of the conversation.

Centuries ago the Apostle Paul had harsh words for both sides of the pulpit. He grieved both the sad state of proclamation and the gerbil-esque attention span of those who received it. How is a preacher to preach so that the word is heard, so that itching ears are scratched, so that God is glorified and God's people strengthened? How do we assemble the words so they might be heard? And what happens if they are?

No one was prepared for the September 11, 2001, terrorist attacks on the World Trade Center and Pentagon. The days that followed were awash with speculation and accusation, fear-mongering and finger-pointing. Every pastor I know was on high alert, offering a listening ear and a safe place for any who needed it. And every pastor I know jettisoned any semblance of a schedule, including sermon preparation. The need for comfort and conversation was enormous, and left room for nothing else.

Congregational Life

It was with a groan that preachers realized on Saturday night that the week's appointed preaching text was Luke 15:1–10. The text opens with these familiar, but suddenly troubling words, "Now all the tax collectors and sinners were coming near to listen to Jesus. And the Pharisees and the scribes were grumbling and saying, 'This fellow welcomes sinners and eats with them.'" What follows are three parables about God's love for the lost: the lost sheep, the lost coin, and the lost son.

Even on an ordinary Sunday, these are challenging words. Luke is happy to remind that Jesus spent most of his ministry with unlikely allies. Had he been more politically savvy, Jesus would have made friends with the local rabbi, courted the wealthy in the congregation, worshipped at the mega-temple. But Jesus went out of his way to irritate these natural partners, poking them about their lack of concern for the poor, their strict adherence to laws without regard for life, their desire to be seen rather than to see. On an ordinary Sunday, we would chuckle knowingly at Jesus' antics, cluck our tongues at the hypocrisy of the Aren't We Right Religious, proudly take our seats beside the tax collectors and sinners who so often graced Jesus' table. It is, after all, sinners like us whom Jesus loves best, isn't it?

But on that particular Sunday, as smoke still curled from the streets of Manhattan and Washington D.C., as anguished parents stood on street corners shouting, "Have you seen my son? He was in Tower 2!" the familiar text about sheep that stroll, coins that roll, and sons who slink into the night took a dark turn. If Jesus was as fond of sinners as he claimed, as hell-bent on seeking the lost as Luke would have us believe, he might well have spent time with the sinners we had met that week, sinners who plotted terror on a massive scale, who dive-bombed death on thousands, who violated everything we believed about safety and security. Suddenly, the sinners with whom Jesus might have broken bread had faces: dark and frightening Arab faces.

In the sermon, I crept tentatively toward the assertion that Jesus' love might include all sinners, even terrorists. I thought my caution was working, that potentially harsh words were softened by thoughtful delivery. But a worshipper in the middle of the assembly realized where I was headed before I spoke the words. Silently he stood, pushed his way down a pew of bony knees and availed himself of the exit. Another followed. Then another. There was no mass exodus, but even those who remained, later took me to task. I can't blame them.

Can You Hear Me Now?

My words that day were completely defensible and textual; I stand by them to this day. But I spoke too soon. It was foolish to imagine we were ready to shed the gospel light on our enemies. It was naïve to believe our congregation was of one mind with regard to the long reach of God's love. It was premature to challenge the of-the-moment belief that all Muslims were to be mistrusted. It was thoughtless to ignore the deep need for comfort. My observations were more suited to later conversation, rather than as a scathing monologue.

In my desire to be faithful to a text, I had been unfaithful to the people in my care. I had read the text, but not the congregation. Much to my chagrin, on that raw and painful Sunday, they heard exactly what I said, and, as soon as the words were out of my mouth, I wish I had not said them at all.

By now you are probably wondering why anyone would be foolish enough to even attempt the preaching task, let alone make it a life's work. As with so many other tasks in work and in life, the preacher must be of two minds at the same time: deadly serious about the preaching task and bemusedly distant from it. How do we strike that balance?

Many years ago I fell into conversation with a woman whose husband and two children had died in a flaming car accident; she was the only survivor. She told me of her search for a congregation to call "home" after that unspeakable tragedy. She had visited churches of every denominational stripe in cities as much as two hours from her home. I asked what she had been looking for in a congregation, what it was she had mostly failed to find. She told me, "I'm waiting to hear a preacher who believes more in life than in death, but who isn't afraid of either."

Every time I am tempted to step into the pulpit with an airy bit of fluff for a sermon, I remember her, and her brutal need for honesty and hope. Though I met her only once, she changed me as a preacher. What I preach matters. In fact, to someone like her who had lost everything dear, it might mean life or death.

That said, we cannot produce a masterpiece every week.

There are weeks or texts or circumstances in which we couldn't produce a coherent sermon if you held a Bible to our heads. Sometimes, in spite of our most ardent efforts, the words don't come, the thoughts don't gel, the text's central issue eludes us. But we preach anyway, confident that, unless the sermon is so bad the gong sounds and the trap door opens beneath us, we get to go another round in the pulpit next week. Those are the weeks when the Holy Spirit does all the heavy lifting, and we gladly relinquish the load.

No preacher preaches powerfully every week. Most of us are lucky to preach well once in a while. In the same way, hearers cannot be expected to carry the whole preaching load—even the most careful listening cannot make something out of nothing. But they bring more to the event when they come prayerfully prepared for whatever word the Spirit sends.

Preacher and hearer are partners in the gospel's work. God's people cannot hear if no one preaches, and there is no preaching unless someone listens. Can you hear me now?

Can You Hear Me Now? Questions for Discussion

1. What is the central dilemma portrayed in this essay?

2. Describe the unique preaching responsibilities of the preacher and of the hearer.

3. How might the preacher "control" the message the sermon intends to convey?

4. How does the congregation encourage and support the preaching task?

5. What topics or circumstances might be better addressed in mutual conversation than in a sermon? Could the Sunday morning worship context ever afford that opportunity?

8

The Little Dunker

Without introduction, the woman on the phone said, "Is this the pastor? Good. We want to have our little dunker done next Tuesday at my grandma's house. There's lunch afterward and you can stay if you want."

I stammered, wondering what I had missed. "I'm sorry. Who is this? Have we met?"

She didn't hesitate. "No, we haven't met. But Grandpa went to a Lutheran church once and everybody is in town for a reunion next week, so we thought it would be fun to have the baby done then. We even found Grandma's baptism dress. How cool is that?"

I had no idea who I was talking to or why she was calling me. I tried to slow the conversation, to get her name and some information, but she very quickly grew huffy with me. She could not understand my hesitation, my questions, my apparent lack of enthusiasm for the opportunity to "do her little dunker." When I asked if we might meet to talk about baptism, she shouted into the phone, "See if we ever come to your church!" and slammed the receiver down.

Please understand. I am happy to talk about baptism with anyone—young or old, believing or skeptical, cemented in a congregation or still seeking. But I don't know many pastors who would agree to an on-demand baptism for complete strangers. And, though I know there are many names for baptism—christening, dedicating, immersing—I've never before or since been asked to "get the little dunker done."

Were we talking about a child or a doughnut?

In the Lutheran church we practice infant baptism, though, of course, a person can be baptized at any age. The emphasis in infant baptism is on God as the "actor," the One who initiates the love, the One who acts on our behalf. Lutherans believe in radical grace, in God's limitless love for us though we are unworthy and undeserving. Baptism is one such means of that grace. We baptize infants as a sign that God loves us regardless of our station in life and before we are able even to ask. When an infant is baptized, the parents and/or baptismal sponsors make promises to raise the child in the faith, trusting that when the child is older he might "affirm" his baptism, taking on those baptismal promises for himself.

Other Christian denominations practice "believer's baptism." In believer's baptism, the baptismal candidate is the "actor," the initiator. He will have attained an age or a maturity level before seeking a relationship with God and the gift of baptism.

In both infant and believer's baptism, words are spoken and water is poured. Neither practice is right or wrong. It is a question of emphasis. Does God take the initiative in the relationship, or do we? Regardless of emphasis, baptism is an important sign, a significant commitment, worth our thought and prayer and preparation.

There was a time in the Lutheran church when, heavily influenced by Roman Catholic teachings about purgatory and under the shadow of high infant mortality rates, baptism was viewed as "insurance" against eternal damnation. Baptism was something to be done as quickly as possible, whether or not the baptized or his sponsors had any intention of living as a baptized person, as a disciple. Certainly, many who were baptized took baptism very seriously, understanding it as a gift from God. But the fear of hell's fires spurred some to the font with greater haste and less intention than we might like.

Lutherans have moved away from the "fire insurance" view of baptism, stressing instead its implications for the way we live. But, as evidenced by the request to "do the little dunker," not everyone buys into this all-inclusive view of baptism. Some view baptism as simply a parental duty, perhaps even a right. These people are not happy when the pastor slows the process with questions or concerns. They respond to our well-intentioned wondering with a strong word and a dial tone.

Congregational Life

I was baptized on a hot June day in my home church in north central Iowa, a thriving country parish, set on a high point among waving fields of corn and soybeans. My grandparents, who helped build the church building, are buried in the church cemetery, as will my own parents when they die. All our relatives, neighbors and family friends were members of that parish. Living out the faith through that congregation was as normal as breathing. Therefore, there was never a question about whether or not I would be baptized. The only question was *when*. Because generations of Lutherans had been taught that baptism "saves" the child, I was baptized as soon as it was possible.

Though I was baptized at only two weeks of age, the impetus for my baptism was not primarily fear. We teach and believe that baptism is a sign—a sign for our sake, a sign of God's welcome and compassion and love for sinners. After all, it is by grace that we are saved, not by some action on our part or our parents' part. My baptism did not save me, but set me on a journey of faith. I acknowledge my baptism anniversary each year, grateful for my parents' faith and for those corn-fed, sunburned, windblown Lutherans who placed my feet on the baptismal path.

When my daughters were born, each of them in the dead of winter, we waited to celebrate their baptisms until Easter morning. After all, Easter is the primary festival of the church, the day on which we speak most clearly about God's power over sin, death, and the devil. We wanted our daughters' baptisms to be part of that ancient celebration of life and hope, for their baptisms to be accompanied by endless Easter "Alleluias!" That meant that our older daughter was four months old when she was baptized, and, nine years later, our younger daughter, five months old.

I was surprised to learn that our decision to delay our older daughter's baptism until Easter was the source of some concern in the congregation. I should have known something was afoot when we were often asked a variation of, "When is she going to be baptized?" Finally, someone blurted, "Why are you waiting? What if something happens? You can't do that to her."

It took me a moment to understand the concern. When it dawned on me that she feared for my daughter's eternal salvation should our little one die unbaptized, I was floored. First, I could not even begin to imagine my newborn's death; it was too horrible to contemplate. Second, I suddenly recognized the implications of the dramatic shift in our church's emphasis about baptism. No longer did we stress baptism as the route to salvation, but as a sign of God's unmerited, limitless love for sinners.

However, my parishioner's comment confirmed that not all of us were on the same page. As calmly as I could, I said, "If my daughter were to die in infancy, it would be a tragedy of unimaginable proportions. I can't even think about it. But, if she were to die unbaptized, I know that God would still welcome her as God's own. She was in God's care and keeping from before she was born, and not even death can change that."

Contrary to what some might fear, no harm is done if a child is not baptized. The unbaptized are not automatically sentenced to an eternity of hell's fires. God does not withhold mercy and love from the "unwashed." God does not review congregations' baptismal records when deciding how to deal with us when we die. When, in Matthew 28, Jesus gives the Great Commission: "Go, therefore, and make disciples of all nations, baptizing them in the name of the Father and of the Son and of the Holy Spirit," there is no implied condemnation of those whom the disciples fail to reach with word and water. Jesus' command is an instruction *for* the disciples, not judgment *against* the unbaptized.

As a colleague tells baptismal candidates, "Baptism is not about what happens if we die. It's about what happens if we live."

I never say "no" to a request for baptism. However, if the request comes from someone who is not a practicing Christian or who is not known to me, I ask that they spend time with us. I ask them to worship with us for six months, get to know the congregation, determine if this is the place they would like to raise their child in the faith. I ask them to engage in conversation about baptism, so they understand the promises they make to their child and the promises the congregation makes to them. If they are unwilling to take that time, to learn more, to keep baptismal promises, I leave it to them to say "no."

Not everyone appreciates this practice.

Some would argue that we should baptize everyone who asks, trusting the Holy Spirit to move their hearts and minds to faithful living. I hesitate to be so indiscriminating. It pains me to watch parents and sponsors perjure themselves, confessing a creed they do not believe, making promises they do not intend to keep. It seems disingenuous for the congregation to pledge its ongoing love and prayers to those who might never brighten the church doors again. And what does it say of the pastor who allows this falsehood to unfold?

Others contend that baptism is a commitment not only to a day but to a life, and engage baptismal candidates, parents and sponsors in an extended program of study, worship and prayer. These pastors will baptize only those who complete this program, who provide evidence of an intention not only to be baptized, but to live a baptized life. I admire these congregations and pastors, but have been mostly unable to make that rigorous practice real in the parishes I have served. Rarely do I encounter baptismal parties who are willing to engage in anything more than a single conversation and a "rehearsal." Some balk even at those minimal expectations.

Most pastors and congregations are able to avoid the outrageous or wacky baptism request. More often we find ourselves vacillating between unquestioning openness and faithful caution. We welcome those who seek baptism, but ask for some sign of intentionality. We trust the Spirit to do its work, but expect honesty on the part of those whom we baptize. There is no "right" way, no surefire method. We are as faithful in our discernment as possible, trusting God to forgive our failures and bless our blunders.

Among pastors there are the outliers, the lone rangers. A pastor of my acquaintance will baptize anyone, anywhere—for a fee. I had a colleague who prided himself on unconventional baptisms. He once baptized a man in the restroom of a bar after a (probably inebriated) confession of faith. He boasts of the water fountain baptism of four teenagers during halftime of a football game.

Though I am cautious and intentional about baptism, I, too, have baptized in unusual or unique situations, but not without planning and preparation. I baptized a wriggling toddler in a cold Wisconsin lake. I baptized an elderly widower the night before he married his also elderly and widowed high school sweetheart. I privately baptized a grade school boy whose cognitive and behavioral disabilities made the prospect of a public baptism nightmarish for him. But such circumstances are the exception, not the rule.

Lent in our parish was a time of focused study, worship and prayer. One year we spent our six weeks of Lent studying, preaching and practicing forgiveness. Another year we analyzed the Lord's Prayer until it begged to be left alone. One year we studied the differences and similarities among the four Gospel accounts of Jesus' passion. One year, since we happened to have multiple baptisms scheduled for Easter morning, the whole congregation studied baptism.

The Little Dunker

We had a lot of fun. We each wrote about our own baptisms, interviewing our parents and sponsors when possible, making contact with the congregations in which we were baptized. We talked about the initiation rites of other religions. We invited a member of the parish who was baptized as an adult to tell us about his faith journey. We spent an evening with the families of those whose children would be baptized on Easter. We studied the development of infant baptismal theology and practice from the early church to the present. We talked about water. And one evening I told about my own baptism, and shared some of the complexities pastors face when asked to baptize.

I was honest about my yet-evolving understanding of what baptism means, of the responsibilities given to the baptized, parents and sponsors, and the congregation. I told them that I made myself uncomfortable with my own questions and concerns. I told them about my policy of inviting baptismal candidates and their families to be part of a congregation and to prepare for baptism. I confessed my frustration with families and individuals who would do anything I asked in order to be baptized, with no intention of keeping their baptismal promises. And I told, in what I thought was a humorous fashion, the story of the "dunker."

Before I had finished the story, Geraldine was on her feet, her finger waving in my face from across the room. "Who made you God? What gives you the right to condemn an innocent baby to hell?"

There was a collective gasp, followed by silence. Geraldine was not finished.

"If there's no harm in baptizing, why not just do it? How many people have you driven away from the church with your smug rules and regulations?"

I tried to take it all in, to listen carefully and, at the same time, craft some kind of cogent response. But Geraldine's upset had sparked a fire. Multiple conversations were happening all at once as people challenged me and one another. One woman made a beeline for the exit and didn't return. Though I was not sure exactly what had happened, it was clear that I had touched a nerve. We took a coffee break, some stepped outside for a smoke, and then we tried again.

I invited Geraldine to tell us more about her concerns. Slowly, tearfully, she began to tell a story from her childhood, about an infant brother who had died before the pastor could baptize him. The child was not named. The pastor and congregation never publicly acknowledged the child's birth or death. Burial was private and outside the cemetery walls. It was as though the child had not existed—on earth or in heaven. Seven decades later, the story still made her weep. Geraldine told us that her father never stepped inside a church again, and that he had asked to be buried outside the cemetery fence, beside his unbaptized son. She told how her mother fell into a stormy silence from which she never emerged.

It did not require any imagination to understand Geraldine's anger with me.

The room was silent as she spoke. Many had tears in their eyes. When Geraldine finished, she looked down at her lap, kneading her arthritic knuckles, fighting tears, relieved and distraught at the same time.

Geraldine had grown up in the church at a time when baptism was viewed as the key to the heavenly gates. Her pastor's failure or refusal to baptize was perceived as a judgment on the whole family. I don't know all the circumstances, and will not speculate about the now-deceased pastor's motives or intentions, but it is fair to say that his actions—or inactions—caused irreparable harm. All her life, Geraldine grieved the brother whom she would never meet, not even in heaven, she feared, all because the pastor did not baptize him.

Most of those who shared Geraldine's anger at me had grown up with the same understanding of baptism as she. To hear me, their beloved pastor, say that I might not baptize was horrifying to them. My nuanced discussion of the pastor's baptism dilemma was lost on them, drowned out by memories of "unwashed" babies and broken hearts.

Lutherans speak of baptism as a "means of grace," one of the primary ways in which God's relentless love and mercy are extended to sinners. It is not a requirement, but a gift, a sign. Baptism is not to be taken lightly, nor is it to be hoarded. How do we speak of God's unwavering love for sinners without cheapening that gift? How do we live the faith with intention and purpose, without becoming rigid or judgmental?

In my ongoing desire to keep the Great Commission, to faithfully speak and demonstrate God's love for the whole world, I return again and again to the words we speak to the newly baptized, their heads wet with water and their foreheads smeared with oil:

> We welcome you into the body of Christ and into the mission we share: join us in giving thanks and praise to God and bearing God's creative and redeeming word to all the world.[1]

1. "Order for Holy Baptism," *Evangelical Lutheran Worship*, 231.

The Little Dunker

Here is where I find myself: Baptism is both an event and a way of life. In baptism, we welcome and we send. We give thanks and we bear witness. We delight that God's word is still creating and redeeming the whole world. These paired understandings continue to guide and challenge my pastoral practice.

To dunk or not to dunk? That is a question for the coffee shop.

Baptism—both the event and the lived reality—demand more serious consideration.

Congregational Life

The Little Dunker Questions for Discussion

1. What is the central dilemma posed by the essay?

2. What sort of requirements, if any, should be held with regard to baptism? Or should baptism be freely offered to anyone who asks?

3. Think out loud about these two divergent views of baptism: baptism as way of life and baptism as a saving event.

4. Tell the story of your baptism. Who baptized you? When and where did it take place? Why were you baptized? Are there any favorite memories of your baptism day?

5. If you are not baptized, describe the decision process that led to that decision.

9

Two or Three

The pool table was shabby, its green felt scuffed and stained, the black bumpers scarred from a thousand beer-botched miscues. The room was smoky, the floor sticky; the whole place smelled of spilled beer and rank restrooms. For many people, this might be an ordinary scene on a weekend—out at the bar on a Saturday night, swapping lies with friends and making eyes at the good-time Charlies at the bar. But this was a Sunday morning, not a Saturday night. And I was the pastor, not a patron. On this occasion, the pool table served as a makeshift altar for a makeshift congregation meeting at the bar nearest the airstrip.

I was serving as pastor in a downtown Anchorage congregation, in a building built low and strong to withstand earthquakes, with a sanctuary large and spare enough to double as a basketball court. Though the congregation was fifty years old, it still had an air of the temporary about it, as if we could pack up and move on a moment's notice. The sanctuary chairs were molded plastic, the floor linoleum tile. The chancel was a carpeted platform on wheels, easily moved from side-to-side or out of the way. For all its temporary-ness, it was a sanctuary, nonetheless, sporting all the requisite furniture: pulpit, table, font. It was unlike any church building I had seen before, but it was church, nonetheless, nestled in the shadow of the Chugach Mountains.

Our parish had the unique privilege of providing pastoral services for a remote Lutheran congregation in a fishing village accessible only by air, 500 flight miles due west from Anchorage. Once a month one of the three pastors on our staff flew there to do in twenty-four hours what usually took a week: teach confirmation, visit the sick, counsel the troubled, prepare the betrothed, meet with leadership, contact newcomers, commune the homebound, preach and preside at worship. We worshipped in the tavern because it was the largest meeting place in the village, unused on Sunday mornings, and, most important, adjacent to the airstrip. The pastoral work began the minute airplane wheels touched down on the narrow tarmac on Saturday midday, and ended with "wheels up" a short day later.

Though exotic to me, the Lutherans there saw nothing unusual about this circumstance. They were adept at making do. They were also completely tuned into those once-a-day flights from Anchorage. Like a dog waking from a sound sleep at the sound of a familiar car in the driveway, the locals perked up when a plane dropped through the clouds. They could tell time by the approaching drone of the propellers, and it was a good thing—our smoke-filled sanctuary had only a flashing neon "Bud Light" clock and, according to "Bud," it was always five o'clock.

Each month when we gathered for worship on a Sunday morning, a member of the parish stood sentinel at the bar's battered front door, one ear tuned to worship, the other to the airstrip. When the airplane's hum thrummed in his ears, the lookout gave the sign, and the pastor quickly wrapped up whatever she was doing. Simultaneously dropping robes, running down the "aisle," throwing on coat and boots, grabbing a bulging overnight bag, the benediction was shouted over the pastor's shoulder as she raced to catch the only flight home that day. The pastor did not stop to catch her breath until squeezed into a cramped seat on a Piper Cub, snug between unshaven fishermen and their finned traveling companions: gleaming sockeye salmon nestled in dry ice.

It might seem unusual to some, this Tavern Temple, but it worked for us. With no church building available to us, we carved holy space out of a cramped saloon. And we offered all that was offered in a "typical" church building on Sunday mornings. Visitors were welcomed. Children were taught. Hymns were sung. Prayers were prayed. The word was preached. The Meal was shared. We lacked for nothing. Nothing but the approval of Lutherans both there and in other places who deemed our makeshift sanctuary "inappropriate." I wonder why.

Jesus said, "Wherever two or three are gathered in my name, there I am in the midst of them" (Matt 18:20).

Two or Three

Martin Luther wrote, "The church is the assembly of all believers among whom the gospel is purely preached and the holy sacraments are administered according to the gospel."[1]

Technically and theologically, there was nothing heretical about our unusual worship location. After all, the people of God are the church when even a few are gathered around the word and sacraments. All three "requirements" were met in that smoky sanctuary. So why the offense?

It seems some of us have conflated two separate issues. The first issue is that of defining what it means to be the church, paying attention to the biblical and doctrinal admonitions that the church is present when we have people, word and sacrament. The second issue is that of "appropriateness." Somehow, to some, it seems more "appropriate" to speak God's name, to share the Supper and pour the water in a building set aside solely for that purpose. While we may dismiss their concerns as small-minded or prudish, we have to take them seriously. After all, these same people who looked down their noses at that fishing village worship situation are our brothers and sisters in the faith and not to be quickly dismissed.

We are attached to our buildings, to our sanctuaries. Sometimes obsessively so. There are some, well-meaning and Jesus-loving, who would add to our three "requirements" for the church the same three things that matter to realtors: location, location, location. More specifically, that the location for worship and congregational life ought to be a dedicated, respectful, beautiful," appropriate" house built for God. With nary a neon beer sign in sight.

Don't get me wrong. I love church buildings. In fact, every congregation I have served has not only had a building, but has expanded and enhanced its building, as well. In one case, the church building needed to be made accessible for the disabled and for children—an elevator project that took on a million-dollar life of its own. In another case, the building was perfectly suited to ministry in 1923, but could no longer accommodate the congregation's staffing needs, technology upgrades, fellowship plans or worship patterns. In yet another parish, the building still looked like the multipurpose room it had once been; it was time to make it "look like church." I have been part of building projects that added floor space, torn down old walls and erected new ones, and tinkered with everything from boiler pipes to organ pipes. And we've spent an enormous amount of money

---

1. Luther, "The Augsburg Confession," *The Book of Concord*, 42.

Congregational Life

and time doing it. So don't imagine that I am dismissive of or a minimalist about church structures. I love a beautiful sanctuary as much as anyone.

Church buildings tend to highlight our "edifice complex." Church building projects, of which I have been an instigator, draw this complex into sharp focus. Given the opportunity to shape a worship space to its own specifications, congregations become rabid with demands and dreams. I will never forget a congregational meeting at which the music director spat, "What are you going to do with the lump under the rug? Because you'll carpet this room only over my dead body." In still another, a mission-minded elder trembled with passion as he challenged, "If we have a million dollars to spend, why aren't we caring for the poor instead of cushioning our own rear ends?"

Fighting about facilities. Does Jesus really care if we speak his name on carpeted floors or on sandy beaches? Are the sacraments more efficacious when offered at hand-carved altars or out of the trunk of a car? Is it a misuse or a faithful use of the church's money to erect walls and install stained glass windows?

We spend much time and energy, anger and anxiety on the buildings in which we worship. But why? It was enough for the ancient Israelites to pray in the desert, with nothing but a tent and an ark to delineate holy space. Jesus chose to preach most frequently in the open air without audio or visual support. The first-century church worshipped and ate in one another's homes. We gustily sing "What is this place where we are meeting? Only a house, the earth its floor."[2] Yet we build buildings, and maintain buildings, and fight over buildings until, sometimes, the only thing we have left is a building.

There is good reason for church buildings, for beautiful sanctuaries and well-appointed rooms. Buildings provide a place to recognize God's presence, giving glory to God's name by creating beautiful spaces in which to worship God, welcoming places in which to greet and feed the poor, warm and safe environs for those violated by the world. All that beauty and dignity and care can be a powerful tool for ministry.

It can also become an idol.

Too many churches exist only as a street address, with a remnant of the faithful drawing down the endowment, plugging holes to keep out the rain. Too many congregations imagine the building and the ministry to be the same thing, that one cannot exist without the other.

---

2. Oosterhuis, "What Is This Place" *Evangelical Lutheran Worship*, #524.

Two or Three

We create an idol any time the protection of a thing or a person or an idea becomes our highest goal. It is idolatry to maintain a building at all costs. It is idolatry to value a structure more than its purpose. A structure, however beautiful or humble, that was intended as a point of contact between God and humanity, too easily becomes the point itself. To misquote scripture, it would be better for that congregation if that precious piece of real estate were thrown into the sea, freeing its inhabitants from the need to worship it.

So why not worship in a tavern? Or on a beach? Or on a battlefield? Or in a living room? And when did "appropriate" become a criterion for worshipping God?

Buildings serve the church. Churches do not serve the building.

The last night of church camp was a carefully scripted, fire-lit, tearstained drama—its script written over decades of camping ministry. As the camp fire's flames snapped in the night air and children's voices rose to the starlit sky, God's presence was as real as the mosquito bites on our sunburned legs. The highlight of the last night's campfire was Holy Communion under the pines. Many young people trace their first experience of Christian community to those quiet nights. Some of them received their first communion in that outdoor sanctuary. Many tears were shed, burdens lifted, sins forgiven. That final campfire was holy time, holy ground for both campers and staff.

We had had a beautiful week at camp that year—the weather was perfect, our campers were a delight, our counselors a pleasure. We played outside from early dawn until long after dark, reveling in snipe hunting, scripture skits, "Capture the Flag," and late-night (mostly unauthorized) canoe rides under the stars. Local weather forecasters predicted that a violent storm front, wind and rain and maybe even hail would move through our area at the end of the week. But, in our sun-drunk delirium, we refused to heed the weather warnings and went ahead with our elaborate plans for our last night around the fire.

Perhaps we should have paid attention to the first distant rumble of thunder. "Trucks on the highway," we assured one another. A thick bank of dark clouds over the western woods was dismissed as "moving too slow to bother us." Even the first heavy raindrops did not deter us. "It will pass." By the time we had ascended the dark campfire hill, singing by candlelight, carrying the little ones already sleeping after a long day outdoors, it had

Congregational Life

begun to rain more steadily. We accommodated the deteriorating weather by singing a little faster, preaching a little shorter, praying with a little less silence.

Staff members and pastors consulted one another as the rain came down more heavily. "We're already wet," was the verdict. But just as we broke the bread and poured the wine, the heavens opened and the rain cascaded down in sheets. We could not see for the downpour, were instantly chilled to the bone, slipped and slid in the mud as the week's best campfire sputtered to steam. We hastily communed one another with soggy bread and diluted wine, sending campers and counselors racing down the hill to shelter as soon as the cup left their lips.

It was fun, we told ourselves. It was an adventure. It was a memory in the making.

Looking back, I now know it was complete foolishness, even hubris, to have made that nighttime trek up the hill. One misplaced lightning bolt, one hurtling hail stone, one fall on a rain-soaked path and we would have a disaster on our hands. But, as they say on the basketball court, "No harm, no foul."

When the senior staff gathered later that night to debrief the week, still with wet heads, chuckling about our daring feat, one of our staff members was livid with rage. "You thought that was fun? It was dangerous! It was foolish! Someone could have been hurt!" I tried to reassure him that no harm had been done, but in my heart I knew he was right. My need to carry on as we always had, my desire to give this crop of campers the Last Night at Camp we had given hundreds of others before them blinded me to the dangers to which we had exposed them.

We had made of that outdoor sanctuary an idol as surely as others do with buildings of marble and mahogany. We had tossed safety, literally, to the wind, violating the most ancient premise of the church as "sanctuary."

Some Christians worship in bars. Some under the stars. Still others in cathedrals venerable and majestic. Which is best? Which is appropriate? Which is safe? Or are these questions we even need to ask about the places in which we gather for ministry?

I wish it were enough for us to believe Jesus' promise of his presence among even a handful of the faithful. I long for a congregation whose highest priority, humbly pursued, is faithful use of scripture and sacrament. I dream of the day when church buildings serve God's people, rather than the other way around.

But we love our buildings. We remember the day the "new" drapes were hung fifty years ago. We name rooms for the dearly departed, making those rooms shrines to the past. Altering worship space, even a smidgen, is tantamount to blowing up Mount Rushmore—unthinkable. And we continue to worship our church buildings, while those two or three of whom Jesus speaks pound on our doors, longing to hear the Gospel and receive the sacraments.

How does this story end? Eventually, the Lutherans in that small fishing village were able to erect and dedicate a church building of their own, leaving the bar and its beer-stained floor behind. That much-loved camping program continues to this day, though with a keener eye to the weather during campfires.

Somehow the church of Jesus Christ—not the building but the reality—continues in spite of us, welcoming sinners, feeding the hungry, healing the sick, preaching the word, washing the repentant. And that church—the church of Jesus's body in the world—has no need of walls or roofs. It is we who need those structures, not God.

Congregational Life

Two or Three Questions for Discussion

1. What is the central dilemma posed by this essay?

2. Why do we erect church buildings? What purpose do they serve?

3. In your opinion, what are primary considerations when designing worship space? For example, a musician might evaluate a church building with regard to acoustics, artists and architects with an eye to visual beauty, engineers would attend to function and ease of maintenance, an environmentalist with concerns for carbon footprint.

4. Describe a church building that might be considered an asset to ministry. Describe another that might be considered a liability.

10

Happy Family

Cut ½ pound chicken meat from the bone.

Beat 5 eggs, dip chicken pieces in eggs and dust with flour.

Reserve egg mixture.

Fry chicken until brown, gradually add mushrooms, sugar, scallions, and onion.

Add fresh spinach.

While spinach is still bright green, pour reserved eggs over all and cook briefly.

Serve over rice.

This is "Happy Family," a Chinese recipe that calls for all parts of a chicken—from beak to butt, as a friend says. It is a delightful dish—a delicious blend of textures and colors, flavors and aromas. It is, indeed, a happy family with the mother and child, the hen and the egg, served on the same plate, baked in each other's juices.

What? Mother and child baked together?

It is best not to think too hard about this recipe. Under too much analysis, the colorful meal on the plate begins to resemble something of a henhouse massacre. Flesh and skin, yolks and whites, fowl mature and embryonic whirled together in a quivering mass of poached poultry parts. I laugh every time I come across this concoction and its inept name. I have to wonder if the eviscerated hen is so pleased to be plated beneath the whipped remains of her inert offspring.

Congregational Life

Happy Family, indeed

Congregations are fond of calling themselves "families." The name is intended to elicit memories of meatloaf and mashed potatoes, fathers-who-know-best and mothers whose spit has healing properties, pretty little children all in a row. But the word *family* can mean a lot of things, not all of them good. Some families are happy and healthy places. But I fear that some of our families bear more resemblance to the broken, beaten, and baked "Happy Family" at my local Chinese restaurant than we care to admit.

While I know that all analogies break down eventually and the concept of a neighborhood Happy Family Congregation is not a bad thing, I still cringe at the language. Congregations are not families. They are congregations. And both entities—the congregation and the family—are plenty hard to plate.

Martha's home was a frighteningly quiet place. Her father worked as a manual laborer, mutely dragging himself home every night with nothing to show for the day but dirty fingernails and a wrinkled paycheck. Her mother didn't hold a job outside the home. She was fully occupied running the home (and Martha's life) with the cool precision of a prison guard.

To say that Martha's mother had control needs is an understatement of a magnitude akin to saying "The Pope attends church regularly." Every paycheck disappeared into the crisp pocket of her apron—neither Martha nor her father ever saw a dime. Martha's clothes were laid out for her every day—even when she was in high school. Meal portions were measured—counted to the pea. Homework was completed with Mother standing over her shoulder, and often rewritten to meet her mother's expectations. Martha's mother timed her walk to school, allowing no dawdling to visit with friends on the way home. Martha's mother cut her hair, clipped her nails, crushed her spirit.

Surprisingly, a harsh voice was never heard in Martha's home; an angry hand was never raised. Martha's was a childhood prison of silent tyranny. Her mother the warden. Her father a mouse in the corner.

Martha did experience one glimmer of hope, one burst of joy in her muted life. After high school graduation, her mother enrolled her at the community college. But a few weeks after classes had begun, a young man called the house asking for Martha. Martha's college career ended that day.

Ended because a love-struck young man made the mistake of trying to break into Martha's constricted world.

Did I mention that Martha's family went to church every Sunday? That they occupied the same pew every week? Did I mention that everyone knew Martha's mother was a tyrant? That Martha's sad life was served up on a platter at every Sunday table in that parish? "Poor Martha," they clucked. "Someone ought to do something." Tongues wagged. Hands were wrung. But Martha remained locked in her mother's relentless clutches.

"Happy Family," anyone?

Congregations bear a tremendous responsibility to provide care for disciples local and far-flung. This is no simple task, and congregations ebb and flow in their ability and willingness to attend to these concerns—ministries both spiritual and physical. This Christ-mandated compassion is further complicated when so much of the needed care is unknown. Baskets of Christmas food for the local poor are a generous gift. Special offerings for distant missionaries are to be applauded.

But what of the child in our own Sunday school who cannot imagine God's love because God's name is nothing more than a curse in her home? What of the man whose wife is immobilized by depression, a man who single-handedly holds home and family together while protecting (and grieving) his wife's illness? Many of our families are something less than picture-perfect; some of them cause harm. Though their needs are never spoken, their sorrows unknown, they are in our care and keeping as well.

Are such sad families well-served by language about "family of God?" An incest survivor flinches every time her pastor speaks of God's fatherly love. Certainly, some fathers are gentle and kind. Her own father's "love" was dark and dangerous. Did God love her that way, too?

I often drive by a church building whose street-side sign boasts "Family Worship every Sunday, 10:30 a.m." Martha won't be visiting there anytime soon. Why would she worship their family when her own is so hurtful?

The children and adults in our care need to know that the church is not simply a replication or endorsement of their twisted family rules. Troubled families keep secrets. Troubled families tolerate bad behavior for the sake of keeping peace. Troubled families manipulate one another for personal benefit. While no congregation intends such ominous overtones when calling itself a family, the person who grew up in a destructive home will insert the implications on their own. A congregation cannot function like these troubled families. Unfortunately, many do, but that is conversation for another day.

Congregational Life

Tentatively, Bill asked Cindy to his senior prom. He was desperately afraid she would turn him down. She was, after all, the prettiest and most popular girl in school. To his surprise, she said yes. Cindy has been saying "yes" to Bill ever since: "Yes, I will marry you." "Yes, I will build a house with you." "Yes, I will raise children with you." Their friends tease them about having a storybook life. Bill and Cindy only smile. Their life is very sweet, and they are very grateful.

Their three daughters, blue-eyed blonde-haired beauties, were born at two-year intervals. In grade school, the girls resembled those nesting Russian dolls—each one a smaller, perfect version of the last. The girls live away now—one in college, two on their own.

Bill and Cindy have had their share of sorrow over the years. Cindy's father died unexpectedly of a heart attack shortly after they married. Cindy's mother moved in with them, helping to raise the children. It was a hard day when Cindy's mother could no longer manage life in their home; she now lives in a nursing home nearby. Bill lost his job in a recent recession, a victim of corporate downsizing. But they scraped their money together, bought a small business and have recovered all they lost. No matter what the trouble, Bill and Cindy held tightly to each other, never letting go of hope or their promises to each other.

My fondest memory of Bill and Cindy is what my husband calls the Midwest Good-bye—Bill and Cindy perfected it. The leave-taking liturgy begins when the last cup of coffee is poured: "We should probably be going." Chairs are pushed back from the table, but nobody actually gets up. It progresses to standing at the door with coat in hand. The good-bye continues with conversation in the driveway. Once the travelers are in the car, the adieu is extended through an open car window, the car's engine running. The good-bye is not complete until the host home is no longer visible through the back car window, the car's occupants still waving wildly into the rearview mirror. Such a good-bye could last forty-five minutes. I have a poignant picture in my mind of Bill and Cindy bidding good-bye to the taillights of our car as they stood on their front porch in dusky light, their arms around each other's waists, waving us safely home.

You will tell me now that such a happy, healthy family is the reason a congregation might call itself "family." Bill and Cindy's family models all that we want our congregations to be: faithful, sturdy, hopeful, welcoming. It is true; their virtues are virtues to which we all aspire.

Happy Family

But even a family as delightful and grounded as theirs has limits. At the end of the day, Bill and Cindy wave their guests away and return to the safety of their own home, their own ways.

Strong families are, of necessity, exclusive. Children must be protected. Property must be maintained. Family traditions must be guarded. This is what good families are supposed to do. Everyone benefits when families maintain healthy limits and boundaries.

Like Bill and Cindy, congregations that view themselves as family are very good to their guests—the occasional visitor who graces the church's table. A hand is extended in welcome, food is offered, stories are told. But at the end of worship, the "family" goes back about its business and the guest drives away. The carefully and lovingly tended boundaries around the congregational family make it difficult for newcomers to find a place. This exclusion is not intentional; it is a natural outcome of a congregation that organizes itself around the model of the family.

A graduate student of my acquaintance observes that even though she has been worshipping in the same congregation for the three years of her graduate studies, she is still on the "guest mailing list," is still invited to "visitors' potlucks," is still considered a welcome outsider. The family/congregation in which she worships is very kind to her. But no matter how welcome the guest, she will always remain nothing more than a guest if the congregation defines itself as a family.

I can feel the hair rising on the backs of necks even as I write. To many of us, the "family" is sacred, much like Mom, apple pie and the Super Bowl. (Did you know there are congregations that cancel worship on Super Bowl Sunday so people have time to prepare for kick off?) We even make light of the trouble in our families, boasting that "our family puts the *fun* back in dysfunctional." Even though the image of family is common in scripture, and much-loved among us, it is a complicated one.

There are other biblical metaphors we might consider.

For example, in the Epistles, the church is often described as the body of Christ, a metaphor useful for the whole church and for a local parish. It is multifaceted, provocative, inclusive in ways some other metaphors are not.

But even this lovely and ancient metaphor can create problems for us. In a culture obsessed with physical beauty, a world in which toddlers don tiaras and being the biggest loser is a good thing, the "body of Christ" conjures up all sorts of uncomfortable issues. The Apostle Paul was not writing about the mythical "perfect" body, the Gorgeous Gladiator or Barbie's

First-Century Sister. He wrote about the anemic, misshapen, arthritic reality of the disciples' shared life. The body of Christ alternately races forward on twitchy teenage legs and hobbles on the bad knees of yesterday's athlete. The body of Christ is sometimes soft in the middle, lazy and out-of-shape, and other times rock hard, disciplined and focused. The body of Christ needs to be fed, growing strong on the rich and delicious banquet spread in God's word, and other times choking itself on the judgmental and smug snacks served up by cultural Christianity. The body of Christ sometimes shows signs of dementia, forgetting who we are and where we were going, more interested in the vaguely remembered past than the messy today or the unseen tomorrow.

Jesus himself was not wild about the "family" image. He rejected sole and unquestioning obedience to family and its limitations. "Who are my mother and brothers and sisters?" he asks. "For whoever does the will of my Father in heaven is my brother and sister and Mother" (Matt 12:50). Of course, he loved his mother and his brothers and his sisters. But not first. Not only. Not blindly. He also loved the sheep for whom he is the shepherd (John 10:11–18); he loved the vines of which he is the vine grower (John 15:1–11); he loved the wedding guests whose thirst he sated (John 2:1–10); he loved the chicks that he longed to gather under his wings (Matt 23:37b).

There is no single image for Christ's church that works in every time and every location. Christ's church is a gathering of the broken, beaten, and battered people of God, seeking both refuge and purpose. Christ's church is a place where the strong care for the weak, where laughter and tears are freely shared, where no one is a guest for long.

Remember, "Happy Family" is only an entrée at a Chinese restaurant.

Happy Family Questions for Discussion

1. What is the central dilemma posed by this essay?
2. What metaphors are commonly used by and about your congregation?
3. Does the name of your congregation have anything in common with the congregation's ministry?
4. Select one of the metaphors from the essay or generated by discussion, and discuss its strengths and shortcomings as a metaphor for your community of faith.

11

Hitching Horses

They were a small enclave of Norwegian immigrants, hopefully deposited in the rolling farm fields of the Midwest. Though firmly planted in the soil of their New Country, they continued to celebrate the ways of the Old Country. They clung to letters from across the ocean, memorizing the words as though they were holy writ. With tears running down their otherwise stoic faces they sang "Jeg er så glad hver julekveld" around the Christmas tree and offered lutefisk ("the piece of cod that passes all human understanding") to their skeptical German neighbors.

In the 1880s this congregation, like many other Norwegian congregations in the United States, was drawn into the Predestination Controversy. Simply put, the controversy was a theological disagreement over the question of whether or not humans have any role in salvation, or if salvation belongs to God alone. That question tore families, congregations, and whole communities to shreds. Our lefse-loving Norwegian neighbors were no exception.

Each side claimed both the theological and real estate high ground, and neither was willing to budge. They finally decided to divide the ten-acre property evenly in two with a one-lane gravel road serving as a demilitarized zone. New buildings were built. New pastors were called. New Ladies Aid Associations were formed. As a final insult, each congregation erected its hitching posts so their own horses' rear ends faced the other church buildings when tethered. Thus, week after week, month after month, year after year, each congregation was greeted for worship by the sweating horses' asses of the other across the road. *"Takk, i like måte."* or "Thanks, you, too."

Hitching Horses

Alphonse and Liza joined our congregation after a long sojourn in the Land of No Church. They were disaffected Roman Catholics, deeply troubled by the "priest scandal" which came to light some years ago. Their faith in the institution of the church and its emissaries was badly eroded, but they missed worship and Christian community and had gone in search of a congregation. They were drawn to our congregation by the liturgy, the preaching, and the hospitality they were shown. They were very clear with me that they were badly bruised and wary of commitment. Could they worship with us, no strings attached? Of course they were welcome. And their "no strings" policy soon gave way to full and joyful participation in our congregation's life.

Alphonse and Liza were more politically and theologically conservative than I, but we spoke easily about our beliefs and differences, respecting one another as thoughtful, faithful people, united by a common purpose. Alphonse and I often needled each other in good humor, engaging in gentle but honest conversation about our disagreements.

At this same time, our national church body was beginning a conversation about human sexuality, providing study materials for congregations. Our congregation worked its way through each of these study documents. We talked about marriage and divorce, cohabitation and masturbation, prostitution and sexually transmitted diseases. Discussion was lively and pointed, respectful and insightful, sometimes uncomfortable. After all, it's not every day that Lutherans willingly talk about condoms. We didn't fight, but there was no consensus either. Liza was at every meeting, brought some sweet treat to share each time, participated fully in the conversations. But as our discussions turned to the church's teaching about sexual orientation, Liza became less vocal and more guarded.

I could tell she had things to say, but was reluctant to say them in the group, so we spoke privately. She said, "From what I can tell, nobody in the group feels the way I do. I figured it was better just to be quiet."

She grew more and more animated as she described her visceral reaction to the very idea of homosexuality. The thought that our denomination might accept homosexuality as "normal" was abhorrent to her. The idea that we might someday bless committed same-gender unions was beyond her comprehension. "This is the way I felt when I first heard about priests abusing boys. I couldn't believe it. I was sick about it. Still am. This feels the same way. I don't know what to do."

The anguish in her soul showed on her face. "I wouldn't hurt you for the world. You know that, don't you?" I nodded. She continued, words falling over each other. "But I don't know how you can just sit there and not say something. The Bible is clear. Tradition is clear. I am not a judgmental person, but this . . ." She paused, turning her face to the window, "this is just wrong."

Liza soon found reasons not to join us, both on Sundays and during the week. Though Alphonse did not share all her concerns, eventually he stopped coming, too. "She's my wife," was all that he said.

I had hoped to keep them close, to bring them back into our fellowship over time. But when I presided at the blessing of a civil union for two women in our congregation, Alphonse and Liza could bear it no longer. The blessing did not take place in our church building, nor did I make a public announcement about it, but these things have a way of becoming known. I received a sad one-sentence handwritten note in the mail a week after the blessing occurred. "I'm sorry, but we can't stay. Liza."

In the 1880s Christians argued about predestination. Before that, we debated slavery. Since then, congregations and whole church bodies have been caught up in questions of biblical interpretation, women's rights, civil rights, reproductive rights, sanctuary for undocumented workers, divorce, apartheid, communion practice, interfaith dialogue, defense spending, and human sexuality, to name only a few.

We disagree and debate about smaller, local matters, as well. I have seen congregations engage in hand-to-hand combat over a change in worship schedule. Church kitchens are a perennial source of conflict in some congregations. Budget meetings last into the wee hours, as each penny becomes a battle. The introduction of a new hymnal sends people fleeing for the exits, muttering about the merits of the old hymnal as they go.

The pastor plays a critical role in times of disagreement and dissent. Though pastors do not have as much power as some imagine, the pastor's attitude and approach to difficult questions set the tone for the congregation's own deliberations. Occasionally, I have seen pastors become the agents of division, pulling whole congregations into their personal battles. More often, pastors try to negotiate conflict with honesty about their own opinions and understandings, and respect for the opinions and understandings of others.

Hitching Horses

I am privileged to have served congregations that work hard to live together in spite of disagreements. We do not brush trouble aside, but stay focused on the mission at hand, refusing to be deterred or detained by issues that, while important, need not divide. But sometimes, for matters of conscience, individuals have chosen to recede from view, to distance themselves, to gradually write themselves out of our story. Their absence is a hole in my heart and in the heart of the church.

Such division in the body of Christ is always painful. Sometimes, in spite of our most faithful efforts, division cannot be avoided. But when the pastor is the occasion for division, it seems to me the pastor is the horse's ass.

I really love parish ministry; I can't imagine doing anything else for a living. But I am keenly aware of things I don't do well, tasks better left to others. I can work my way through a financial statement, but am no accountant. I read music and sing, but Broadway isn't pounding on my door. I can identify the business end of a hammer, but there is a reason we have a property committee. I manage staff and run meetings and write reports and even clean a toilet now and then, but my real love and my gifts are for general parish ministry. Preaching, teaching, caring for the sick, presiding at worship, working with volunteers—that's what I do best, what I love.

Over the years I have learned to do my pastoral tasks well, and to empower and trust others to use their gifts for ministry. So, while I participate in all facets of the congregation's life, I try to leave budgets and contracts and downspouts and soup suppers to those more suited than I.

But every once in a while I forget my place, and step in where I ought not go. One particular instance of this overstepping still makes me cringe, and is a painful reminder of the power of the pastor to divide.

The details of the event are too complicated to relate here, but the broad issue is this: the parish I served was landlocked, right in the middle of a busy downtown. We had a policy that as adjacent properties became available, we would buy them. Though we had no particular purpose in mind for additional land, we believed that real estate is a good thing to own.

I learned through the neighborhood grapevine that an old house near our church was going to be sold when the owner retired to Florida. The owner would have lots of suitors, so we needed to act quickly. After making a telephone call to the congregation president who said, "Go for it," I made a point to run into the homeowner while I was out for a walk. We chatted over the fence. I told her I had heard she was moving, that we would miss her as a neighbor. I hinted that we might be interested in the property. She confirmed both her intended move and the sale of the house. She said she would be happy to entertain an offer from the congregation. "You've been good neighbors. I know you would take good care of it," she said.

The congregation president called a meeting of the executive committee to get the go ahead on our plan. With their approval in hand, we called a local real estate agent to help us make an offer. Within a week everything was settled, and we were ready to call a congregational meeting to approve purchase of the property. It couldn't have been more simple.

Au contraire.

There was a small faction in the congregation that seemed always to regard me with suspicion; I felt they never warmed up to me. I am not sure how it happened, but they seemed to take delight in finding fault with me—putting the worst possible construction on my words and actions. You can only imagine how quickly they jumped on this hasty real estate decision.

And they were right to do so. In spite of my good intentions and the tacit approval of congregational leadership, real estate decisions are not the pastor's to initiate. We had a strong leadership team and a purchase policy in place. We were well-liked in the neighborhood and would have had no trouble buying the property. It might have taken longer to work the parish process, but the outcome would have been the same. I had forgotten my place.

My detractors leapt at my lapse. The accusations were harsh:

Pastor is power hungry.

Pastor disrespects congregational leadership.

Pastor has too much access to church finances.

Pastor made the congregation look bad in the eyes of the neighborhood.

Pastor plays favorites in the congregation.

Admittedly, I had made a serious mistake in spearheading a real estate deal. But this mistake, like most others I make as a pastor, had nothing to do with hunger for power or any of the other things of which I was accused. I just didn't think. The fact is that I can be impulsive, quick to make decisions but slow to consider consequences. I like a challenge, love to fit puzzle pieces together. That impulsivity and delight in challenge have gotten me in trouble more than once. But I would never intentionally circumvent parish process or create division. I don't have the stomach for it.

Within days, my accusers had circulated a petition calling for a congregational vote—ostensibly about the real estate deal, but actually in hopes of undermining me. I later learned that many who had signed the petition were not aware of the real issue, that the accusations against me had been veiled. When they learned the facts of the case, most of the signers asked to have their names removed, but it was too late. The parish leadership was sick about it, as was I, but a petition is a petition, and a congregational meeting had to be called.

I offered to resign my call, rather that put the congregation through a potentially divisive fight, but my offer was refused. "We need to let this play out," the congregation president advised.

I did not attend the meeting. If people had things to say, they needed to feel free to do so. It was the loneliest hour of my life, as I waited in my office to learn the outcome of the referendum on me.

It is naïve to imagine that a congregation will never have conflict, will always get along and move forward in ministry as a single, cohesive unit. Pastors and people have different priorities and passions, different operating protocols. In every parish there are the "persistent troublemakers," who delight in fanning the flames of dissent. Every pastor missteps, misreads and miscalculates. Pastors are often lightning rods for strong feelings, alternately loved and hated more than is deserved or reasonable.

It is not the fact of conflict or disagreement that is the problem. Nor should it surprise us that pastors and parishioners are passionate about ministry, about scripture, about issues, about congregational life. Sadly, however, we are not always on our best behavior, functioning at our most reasonable and gracious.

Congregations and clergy falter in their ability to manage conflict when the discussion turns from the issue at hand to the personal, when the conflict becomes an opportunity to settle an old score or nurse an old wound. As in marital and family fights, you know you're in trouble when your partner starts a sentence with "You always—" or "I'll never forget that time you—" Then the disagreement is no longer about the disagreement, but about the person. And nobody wins.

Of course, some disagreements go beyond the boundaries of acceptable behavior or honest debate. Over the years, I have encountered the parish member who not only dislikes me, but actually seeks to do me harm. Two times my life has been threatened by a parishioner. Lies and rumors about me have been circulated. I have been stalked. Angry and unkind words have been lobbed at me in public settings. Intentional attempts have been made to publicly humiliate me. Copies of my written work have been shredded, defaced and mocked. This behavior is more than simple disagreement. It is sinful and dangerous disdain for a sister in Christ. But it happens.

How does the pastor think about those who actively wish her harm? Long ago I decided that, at the end of each day, I had to be enough at peace with my enemies that I could attend to them in a crisis, that I could be their pastor in an emergency, and tend to them without hesitation. I have striven to so guard my words and actions, to so train my heart that, should the phone ring in the middle of the night, I could rush to my enemy's bedside with a clear conscience and sincere concern for their well-being. It's not easy, but I try.

In Philippians 2:2–15, the Apostle Paul writes that the congregation at Philippi is to "be of one mind." He uses the unusual Greek word *sumsuxoi* which can also be translated "united in spirit" or "to be in harmony." He does not mean that they are to agree about every jot and tittle, or, conversely, brush trouble under the rug. They are to find that place where they desire what God desires, where their love for one another makes disagreement life-giving, rather than lethal.

Note that Paul is not tossing out that tiresome cliché about "agreeing to disagree." All that means is that we regard the other as not worth our time, that their concerns are pointless, and that we are beyond persuasion, regardless of the other's ideas. Paul challenges us with something far more difficult. How might a Christian community "be of one mind" and yet disagree?

Since the presence of disagreement is inevitable, it is incumbent on the pastor to set the tone, model the method, guide the discussion toward mutual understanding, good process, and faithful life.

Writing about Alphonse and Liza fills me with sadness. I cared deeply for them. I grieved the outcome of our disagreement. When we ran into each other at a social event a year after our parting, we hugged happily and then drew away quickly as though burned, reminded of the division between us. Would it have been possible for them to share their disagreements and stay? Did my own beliefs, both about human sexuality and the importance of honoring the multiplicity of views, drive them away? What is our responsibility to those who love the church but cannot agree with some of its teachings?

As painful as that process was, it was as productive and healthy as disagreement can be. Views and values were shared in an environment of respect and care. Disagreements were not personal, but about an issue—an issue on which we, finally, could not find common ground. As much as I miss Alphonse and Liza, I remember them as models of respectful, faithful disagreement. While the congregation was willing to enfold them, they were unwilling and unable to remain in the fold.

Sometimes disagreement divides. But it need not destroy.

I also learned a great deal from my ill-advised and unhelpful foray into the real estate market. I had inserted myself into a process that was not mine to lead. My actions gave credence to the fear of some that I was power hungry. Rather than discussing the issue at hand, it turned into a referendum on me. My accusers were eager to jump on my leadership lapse, but the final fault is mine—I opened the door to dissension and they gladly walked through it.

It would be easy to regard those with whom we disagree as little more than horses' asses aimed our way. But even those with whom we are at odds are brothers and sisters in Christ. I would like to believe that most often disagreements are born of love for the church and its mission, that our struggles are about how best to be faithful to our mission, and not a thinly veiled attempt to misrepresent or harm or condemn.

I might also put in a plug for the Eighth Commandment, the biblical mandate that we put the best construction on another's words and actions. This commandment might helpfully inform all our conversations, making even disagreement less disagreeable.

A wise pastor knows her place in tense times. A wise pastor promotes honesty, kindness, focus, and fairness. A wise pastor knows where best to hitch a horse.

Congregational Life

Hitching Horses Questions for Discussion

1. What is the central dilemma posed by this essay?

2. Is agreement necessary for unity within the community of faith?

3. When might it be appropriate to avoid or delay discussion of difficult issues for the sake of "keeping the peace?" What are the dangers of doing so?

4. How does a congregation determine when opposition is borne of faithful disagreement, and when it is merely axe-grinding or troublemaking?

12

Last Gasp

The parish was established in the nineteenth century by German and Eastern European immigrants, drawn to the community by factory work similar to the textile work they knew in their home countries. The congregation became a home for subsequent waves of immigrants, who gravitated to the congregation for familiar food and language and song and dance. Though the original immigrants have long since died, the congregation still identified itself as the "German church" in town.

I grew up in a German immigrant congregation in the Midwest so I imagined myself well-versed in the ethnic traditions. But when I became the pastor of this faith community, I was introduced to German traditions of which I knew nothing. These Germans drank beer; my German ancestors were teetotalers. These Germans danced heel-blistering polkas; my German ancestors played baseball on the church lawn. These Germans gorged themselves on sausage and kraut; my German ancestors slurped oyster stew and erected architecturally stunning Jell-O salads. The most foreign of this new congregation's German traditions was Fastnacht.

"Fast Night" is a German Mardi Gras, an Eastern European Shrove Tuesday. It is a last hurrah, a wild night of drinking and dancing and storytelling before the austerity of the season of Lent. And, as they say, "What happens at Fastnacht, stays at Fastnacht."

Upon my arrival, the old-timers in the parish regaled me with gleeful stories of Fastnacht. They proudly displayed yellowed Polaroids of lederhosen-clad polka bands, of couples swirling across the dance floor, of tables breaking under the weight of sauerbraten and red cabbage and fatal desserts. They disagreed about the number of kegs consumed each year, but

Congregational Life

all remember that the event was awash in imported German ale. They were most proud of the Fastnacht plays—original dramas produced each year by an impish, daring team of writers who, with a wink and a nod, strained the boundaries of acceptable behavior and good taste.

Actors wore outlandish costumes, some risqué and others pompous. They strung zip lines across the stage ceiling, and erected elaborate sets to enhance each year's drama. The script dripped with puns and sexual innuendo and groaning biblical jokes. The cast included a few regulars each year, but they always invited new members and friends into the fun—unsuspecting but cheerful victims of Fastnacht nonsense.

Fastnacht required months of writing and scheming, menu-planning and sewing. The event was standing room only, with requests for next year's tickets coming in almost before the curtain was drawn on this year's play. At least, it used to be that way.

By the time I arrived, the original instigators of Fastnacht had died, or were so old they couldn't join the fun anymore. A new generation of congregational members, with no ties to Germany or its traditions, regarded Fastnacht as an amusing but mystifying oddity. Bottomless beer kegs and ribald behavior were frowned upon as a bad example for the youth, and a legal liability. Attention had turned to the practices of Lent, rather than the preamble to it. Little by little, Fastnacht was losing its luster.

However, a small group of the Fastnacht Faithful remained, so we gamely soldiered on. I donned a black cassock and mustache to play Father Guido Sarducci (see *Saturday Night Live* circa 1978) in the play my first year. The kitchen crew worked for days to prepare the traditional German feast. The fellowship hall was festooned with streamers and balloons and cardboard cutout beer steins.

But the crowds did not materialize. The polka band was booked elsewhere. What had been billed as a wild night of pre-Lent hilarity was a subdued, modestly attended congregational dinner, interrupted by a silly one-act play and halfhearted dancing.

My heart hurt for the planners, and for those elderly immigrants for whom Fastnacht was a last link to home and family. Fastnacht was a great event that had lost its *reason d'être*. Sadly, I presided over the last gasp of Fastnacht a few years later. Though it was hard, the decision to lay Fastnacht to rest was a mutual one, carefully reasoned and clearly communicated. We all recognized that, while Fastnacht had a long and proud history in our parish, it was not central to our mission. It was fun, but could not be our focus.

Last Gasp

∽

Lucia Brides and Christmas Bazaars. The choir's reverent singing of "The Palms" on Passion Sunday. Run away when someone says, "We always—."

Some shake their heads and grieve that "times have changed," that there is no respect for the way things used to be. Others bemoan the loss of community spirit, of the desire for a congregation to gather just for fun. The True Believers are more critical of congregational change, believing the "abandonment" of church traditions to be thinly veiled criticism of the people and practices that once drove the congregation's life.

These mourned traditions can be simple—the accepted arrangement of tables in a fellowship hall, or the size of the pots for the Easter lilies. Others are complicated—idiosyncratic organizational structures or patterns that have become a hindrance to ministry rather than a help.

It is very hard for congregations to accept that all events and structures have a shelf-life, a best-if-used-by date, a beginning and an end. Every pastor cringes upon hearing the Seven Last Words of the Church: "But we've always done it that way." Too often, the last gasp a congregation hears is not the necessary dying breath of a beloved-now-bygone tradition, but the whispered good-bye of parishioners (and sometimes pastors) for whom the congregation's remembered-past is a burden they do not share and can no longer bear.

Traditions are not inherently bad or destructive. Traditions are a way we teach the values of our congregations, a way we welcome newcomers to our ministry, a valuable link to people and events that enriched the congregation's life in the past, a thread running through the congregation's life. It is possible for long-standing traditions to be fun and welcoming and purposeful. But that doesn't happen by chance. Even the most venerable congregational event requires regular and honest evaluation. We need to ask:

How does this event reflect our congregation's values and goals?

Does this event welcome people or discourage their involvement?

Whose needs are being met by continuing this event?

Is this event a blessing or a curse, a blast or a burden?

More critically, does this event further our mission or is it merely a distraction?

Congregational Life

> It requires great wisdom and courage for congregations and pastors to find the balance between honoring those who came before and keeping the focus on what lies ahead.

The Sunday School Movement originated in England in the 1750s, migrating across the pond to the United States in the 1790s. The movement's purpose was to provide formal education for child laborers who had only one day off a week, who had no access to learning opportunities. As child labor laws changed and public education became the norm, Sunday School morphed into multigenerational, specifically Christian education in parishes of all denominations. No longer did children learn to read and write in Sunday school; they learned Bible stories and Christian songs and faith-inspired patriotism.

Sunday schools boomed in the 1950s in this country, as post-war birth rates soared and families sought the respectability and social opportunity of church membership. A whole industry grew up around producing Sunday school materials for congregational use. Congregations built buildings and hired professional staff to direct the millions of children who learned about Noah's Ark with flannel figures and who obediently sang "Onward Christian Soldiers" with no idea that they promoted a militaristic view of Christianity which would soon fall out of favor.

But times really do change. I will not add to the countless studies that have tried to explain current changes in church attendance and involvement. I will not lay blame for changes in congregational life, as some do, on a burgeoning sports culture or emerging social structures or changing family life. Why people worship or study the faith or join congregations is a long, complicated, and nuanced conversation which I am neither equipped nor willing to engage in this essay. It is enough to say that Sunday school and worship and congregational life are no longer the attractions they once were.

But if you thought bidding farewell to Fastnacht or the Annual Mother's Day Tea was fraught with peril, imagine tinkering with Sunday school.

Every Sunday morning I raced from worship to the lower level fellowship hall to open Sunday school. We were privileged to have a large cadre of volunteer teachers and musicians who worked with our children. The pastor's task was to introduce the theme for the day, to bring a biblical story to life or make a link between the children's lives and that day's lesson. I got to receive the children's sticky coins as they made their penny-a-year birthday offering to our Sunday School outreach project. I loved spending time with the Sunday school children and staff—it was often the highlight of Sunday morning.

No one remembers when the change began to occur, but we noticed our children's attendance numbers slipping. Parents were unwilling to commit to a whole semester of teaching, but preferred volunteering a week at a time. The Christmas pageant, formerly a wild but well-rehearsed romp through the Nativity story, was downscaled to accommodate fewer children and minimal rehearsal time. Within the span of a couple of years, we went from welcoming scores of grade school children to our Sunday morning education program to celebrating a handful of very young children who might or might not show up.

The first real acknowledgement of the change was a candid conversation with a young family. "We love Sunday school, but it's hard to convince our kids to come when they are the only ones in their class." The finance committee questioned the amount budgeted for Sunday school materials, since most of the materials we ordered or produced went unused. Our Sunday school teachers, many of them professional educators during the week, tired of planning lessons for which there were sometimes no learners. We experimented with rotational Sunday school and weeknight Sunday school and family-driven Sunday school, with covenants and sticker charts and field trips. But the trend continued downward, as the frustration spiraled upward.

Finally, after trying everything from bribes to babysitting, with dwindling numbers of children, frustrated parents, and a demoralized teaching staff, we decided to err on the side of honesty. We were pouring huge amounts of time, energy and prayer into a ministry its intended audience didn't appreciate. We were catering to the needs of a generation no longer involved with Sunday school, but who insisted it had to continue as it had when their now-middle-aged children were young.

We took a bold step. We did not abandon the program, nor did we forge stubbornly forward. We bought time. Time to plan, to pray, to study, to think. We instituted a sabbatical from Sunday school.

Congregational Life

There is one significant difference between burying an ethnic event like Fastnacht and putting a toe tag on a ministry like Sunday school. The difference has to do with mission. Fastnacht is fun. Fastnacht evokes fond memories. But Fastnacht is not integral to the church's mission.

Conversely, for generations, the church has held that the education of children is of central importance. Though no longer tied to its original purpose of providing general education for poor urban children, Sunday school has been the primary vehicle for teaching our children about the love of God in Jesus Christ. Sunday school serves the multiple missions of evangelism, hospitality, education, outreach and fellowship. It is more than a riotous romp; Sunday school matters.

Remember, Jesus even mandated his disciples to teach: "Go therefore and make disciples of all nations, baptizing them . . . and teaching them all that I have commanded you" (Matt 28:19–20a). There is no such biblical admonition to drink beer or wear funny pants.

Here is the critical distinction: Sunday school both *is* and *has* a mission. That mission has not changed. However, the method is another matter. When we are able to untangle the Mission from the Method we can decide if and how to move forward with this or any other ministry.

Examples from other disciplines:

Ford Motor Corp. pushed the first Model T off the assembly line in 1908. Though within twenty years that particular model was eclipsed by new technology, Ford continues in its mission of making automobiles. Just not the Model T.

Nations have waged war against one another for millennia. However, if in this century an army came to battle on horseback, it would be annihilated in seconds. The dark mission of war is subjugation of an enemy. We still do that, but not on horses.

Abraham Lincoln did his homework by the fireplace, scratching chalk on slate. Chalk has been replaced by dry erase markers, and firelight by the flickering light of a computer screen. Children still go to school. Teachers still assign homework. But not in log cabins.

History is ripe with tales of industries and ideas and innovations that either survived or succumbed. What is the difference between the historical victors and the victims? Faithfulness to Mission, rather than Method.

I'm not saying that the church is a factory or a battle or an educational method or a design concept. I am saying that when we are married to the method rather than the mission, failure, disappointment, and division are almost certain.

Last Gasp

There is another, smaller but important matter to consider that muddies our musings.

The very notion that congregations exist for the sake of mission is a foreign concept to many. Too often we mistake the ethnic tradition, the favorite hymn, the aging elder as our reason for being. We erroneously believe that events and programs have to continue because they are fun, or are long-standing, or because they matter to an individual or a group. How do you tell the dearly beloved patriarch, the hardworking committee, the well-meaning volunteer that the "M" in Mission does not stand for "mine"?

For some, Fastnacht was not only a much-loved German tradition, it was Somebody's Signature Event. In some places Sunday school is not only a ministry of the church, it is "Mabel's Baby" or "Elmer's Passion." In such cases, the distinction between pet projects and the congregation's ministry is dangerously blurred. How do we evaluate the value of a ministry if, in so doing, it seems we are evaluating the value of a person?

Congregations, like all organizations, govern themselves by a set of mutually agreed-upon priorities and tasks. Too often the stated mission bears no resemblance to the actual mission. No congregation would officially adopt the following mission statement: "We do whatever Mabel and Elmer want us to do." But many congregations stumble onward with just such a narcissistic, poorly focused, and badly communicated plan.

If a congregation's highest priority is to honor the dearly departed, or to keep things as much the same as possible, it may reap the benefits of stability, but it will also suffer the ravages of irrelevance. If, on the other hand, the congregation abandons all traditions, it risks becoming addicted to novelty, chasing fads the way dogs chase cars. Which is worse? Cement shoes or rudderless wandering?

However, if the congregation's priority is to faithfully and intentionally minister in its context and community, projects will come and go, leaders will emerge and recede, budget line items will be added and deleted while the mission remains strong. It is a more-than-unsettling way to do ministry, but the only way that leads to new and lasting congregational life.

We are grateful for the past. We are open to the future. As long as we cling to our mission, both things are possible. But they do not happen by accident.

At the end of the day, a congregation needs to decide if it intends to gulp new and bracing air, or take its last gasp.

Congregational Life

Last Gasp Questions for Discussion

1. What is the central dilemma posed by this essay?

2. Does your congregation have a working, site-specific plan for its mission? How and how often are those plans reviewed and revised?

3. How does your congregation evaluate particular events or ministries?

4. Name one "tradition" in your congregation that you cannot imagine ending. When and why was it started? What function does it now serve? What would happen if it were shuttered?

13

Miss Mary

The front pew belongs to children. Rather than being hidden and shooshed to the back rows of our sanctuaries, little ones crave seats front and center. From that privileged perch, they are undistracted by the wiggling and yawning, the comings and goings of latecomers. Children find themselves immersed in worship. They see every expression on the preacher's face. The congregation's song rolls over them like mighty waves. They are the first to whom ushers come seeking gifts for the poor. The great parade of beggars seeking bread and wine passes right by, near enough to touch. There is no need for "children's time" if all our children are in the front—the whole service belongs to them. With the congregation behind, and the ministers before, our children learn to worship in the midst of that great cloud of witnesses.

The front row is the best seat in the house. It belongs to children.

My older daughter was born when I was serving a youthful, child-rich congregation. She was one of five babies born in the same month—it was a fertile place. From her earliest days in worship, while I made my place in the chancel, she and my husband sat in the front row. Sunday after Sunday she munched Cheerios, right under the preacher's nose.

My daughter was just a toddler when I took a new call to another congregation. This new congregation met in a beautiful building, its magnificent spires visible for miles around.

There were many differences between the two parishes, but perhaps the greatest was the *feel* in worship. The first sanctuary was utilitarian—plastic stacking chairs lined up in rows on a functional linoleum floor. The chancel was moveable, the light fixtures member-made. The humble

Congregational Life

furnishings were testimony to a very young congregation, people on the move. By marked contrast, the sanctuary used by the second congregation was a marble cathedral. Every detail of the woodwork was meticulously carved. The stained glass windows cast a holy indigo and amber glow on the faces of worshippers. Pristine terrazzo floors, gleaming gold inlay on the reredos, long oak pews polished to a soft sheen by the expensive suits and soft furs that had filled them for generations.

But, even in a cathedral, the front pew belongs to children.

I was blindsided when, just a few weeks into my call to the stunning church, a complaint came to me through another staff member. Some who wore the expensive suits and soft furs were offended that a toddler would be in worship. That she was in the front pew was an unspeakable affront. "She belongs in the nursery." To drive the point home even further, one of those offended proffered the threat that strikes fear in every pastor's heart, "If she stays, I will go." To be sure, this congregation was a fancier place than the church I had left—older, more refined, wealthier. But a church where children were not welcome in worship?

My husband and I were dumbfounded. We had no desire to offend the members of my new congregation. But we did not understand how the presence of a small child might drive others away. Perhaps this was a custom of which we were unaware: children both not seen and not heard.

The next Sunday, before my husband and daughter entered the sanctuary, understandably nervous about where to sit, he felt a gentle hand on his arm. It was Miss Mary, a diminutive woman who had greeted us when we arrived, but had been silent since. With no explanation or preamble she softly said, "Come, sit with me."

Everything about Miss Mary was soft. She wore her wispy white hair in a cottony bun on the crown of her head. Her voice was pure honey; she knew how to be nothing but kind. In my memory, Miss Mary always wore light blue, almost the same color as her smiling eyes. Though she had been a member of the congregation for decades, most did not notice her. Miss Mary did not command attention, only smiles.

Miss Mary guided my husband and young daughter down the center aisle to the heart of the sanctuary and seated them on either side of her in her customary place. She nodded quietly and without apology to those

Miss Mary

around her. Her pew neighbors were a little surprised; they had imagined their pursed-lipped disapproval would have resolved this little problem.

That morning, as Miss Mary's white head and my daughter's pig-tailed one bent over the same hymnal, the congregation's balance of power shifted. Miss Mary's was not the power of wealth or position, but the quiet, immutable power of kindness. She and my little one sat together only that one Sunday—one Sunday was enough. Her oh-so-civil disobedience gave my family permission to resume their seat in the front of the sanctuary every Sunday after. Miss Mary had done what she needed to do. Besides, that sacred seat at her side would be occupied soon enough, by another unwelcome child.

In spite of that rough start, it was a wonderful congregation. The staff worked hard and well together. The congregation had a real heart for mission, serving the homeless and working poor in our kitchen five days a week. They were heavily involved in neighborhood improvement. Worship was beautiful and thoughtful and rich, welcoming both rich and poor. Our members drove many miles to be part of this thriving city congregation. But for all our outreach efforts and good intentions and community care, there was one neighborhood population we could not reach: The Loiterers.

In spite of the city's best efforts, the congregation's neighborhood was a favorite gathering spot for drug dealers, prostitutes, pan handlers and runaways. The paths of our parishioners and these sometimes seedy neighbors rarely crossed, but we were always aware of them and the security risks they posed.

One Sunday morning, just minutes before worship, one of our ushers stepped into my office to say: "There is someone here who needs to see you." A little annoyed at the interruption of my pre-worship routine, I looked up to see a very tall, very dark-skinned woman in a very tiny skirt standing in my doorway. With a trembling and oddly deep voice she said, "I need your help. He hurt me." Very quickly I realized that the woman before me was not a woman, and that the one who had hurt her was a surprised and angry "john" who had been shopping for sex. The customer's surprise had turned to anger when he discovered the woman for whose services he had paid was a man. He left bruises to register his displeasure at being duped. Makeup ran down her face in dark, tear-stained streaks. She twisted around to show me her ripped skirt. "Can you help me?" she asked. "I can't go back out there like this." I was not sure what sort of help to offer her, but it was clear that, at the very least, her skirt needed repair.

I escorted her into the lobby of the church building to seek help (and to foist her onto someone else). The first person I saw was Miss Mary. "Miss Mary," I said, "this woman has torn her skirt. Could you help her fix it?"

Without blinking an eye, Miss Mary moved her beige handbag onto her left arm, put the prostitute's hand on her right and said, "Come with me." As gracefully as though strolling to lunch, Miss Mary and the prostitute strolled to the ladies' room. When I checked on them a moment later, Miss Mary was standing behind the woman, pinning her skirt shut with safety pins. (Who knew Miss Mary kept an endless supply in her bag?) The prostitute was so tall and Miss Mary so small that Miss Mary did not need to bend to do her mending. She worked at eye-level on the prostitute's backside. Other women who chanced into the restroom did not stay long. One fled the restroom with a look of panic. "There's a man in there! He's wearing a skirt!"

I should have known Miss Mary would not stop with safety pins. This torn and tearful prostitute needed more than that. Leaving the safety of the restroom behind, accompanied by the organist's processional music, Miss Mary guided a very tall, scantily dressed woman with five o'clock shadow to sanctuary. Excusing herself and her guest for being late, she slipped into her place—patting the seat beside her to prepare it for her guest, this older child in distress. Admittedly, the prostitute's reception from her fellow worshippers was cool, but no one challenged her place in worship. After all, this woman was Miss Mary's guest and Miss Mary's hospitality was unassailable. To sit at her right and left was a place of honor to which only the least worthy were invited.

With a strategically placed safety pin and a quiet word, Miss Mary upset the very foundations of that old and venerable congregation. Who had more power that day? The well-heeled, well-bred, well-respected power brokers or the small-statured, small-voiced, big-hearted Miss Mary?

It may come as a shock to some, but congregations are all about power. We like to imagine they are about God's power. But more often they are about human power and human will and the human need to control. Power in congregations is often exerted by those with the most money or the loudest voice or the longest membership or the most ominous threats.

Examples of the misuse of power are almost too many to name. Many congregations suffer the "Back to Egypt" Committee—those who, like the

Miss Mary

Israelites wandering in the wilderness, remembered the good old days, the way it used to be, back home in Egypt, conveniently forgetting four hundred years of slavery under Pharaoh (Num 11:5). I have endured more than one Parking Lot Committee—those who sit silently through council or congregational meetings, only to convene the "real" meeting outside by their cars. Every congregation harbors a Doorknob Queen (or King)—the person who just "stops by" to chat and on the way out, one hand on the doorknob, tosses a grenade: "I just thought you should know—." A colleague who once served a parish rife with naysayers and second-guessers quipped that he was only a few funerals from having a really good congregation. Every pastor can tell tales about the folks who show up only to vote against progress, about people who tell lies and manipulate facts and work behind the scenes to create dissension. Such committees and individuals can be enormously powerful, even dangerous.

Power well-used is harder to find, more difficult to grow. Power well-used builds up and expands ministry. Power carefully wielded invites creativity and thoughtfulness. People and committees of faithful power build buildings and teach children and run meetings and pour coffee and fold newsletters and feed the grieving and serve on committees and worship faithfully and mow lawns and pray unceasingly and forgive freely and care for the world's poor. Theirs is the power of generosity and faithfulness and honest work. But even those examples of well-used, well-meant power don't describe the force behind ninety-pound Miss Mary.

What do we say of Miss Mary? Without serving on a single committee or voicing her opinion at a single annual meeting, Miss Mary was velvet-gloved courage in that congregation. Hers was the power to welcome a stranger, to silence the naysayers, to commit outrageous and delicate kindness.

In the heart of a city pulsing with financial power and historic significance, on a street known for its beauty and wealth, in a congregation known for its articulate preachers and blue-blood pedigree, Miss Mary was welcoming children and pinning prostitutes back together.

Congregational Life

Miss Mary Questions for Discussion

1. What is the central dilemma posed by this essay?

2. What was the source of Miss Mary's power?

3. Who holds power in your faith community? What is the source of that power?

4. Is it possible for multiple sources of congregational power to be exercised at the same time?

14

We Are Not Worthy

Moaning as he rocked back and forth, clapping his hands wildly against his head, it was hard to know if Brad was delighted or distressed. Severely autistic, Brad knew only one way to express himself; it was up to us to interpret.

Brad and his family started their life with our congregation in the back pew, nearest the exit. Their first Sunday it was only ten minutes before Brad started rocking, clapping and vocalizing. A new place. New people. Organ music. It was all too much for him, the sensory stimulation like bombs going off in his head. But the next Sunday they stayed for fifteen minutes; the next they were able to stay almost twenty.

It was a triumphant day when, after many Sundays of growing comfort, Brad came forward for a blessing at the communion table. His parents, Martha and Nick, had coached us in communicating with Brad, when introducing a new thing to him. Brad walked hesitantly to the front of the sanctuary, his mother's arms wrapped around him like a blanket, keeping constant and familiar body contact. I did not try to look him in the eye, touch him or step too close, but I was able to speak words of blessing over his bobbing head. With delight, he clapped and moaned all the way back to his seat.

I knew little about autism spectrum disorder before I met Brad and his family. I knew even less about the barriers the church unknowingly places in the path of those with special needs. But they were patient teachers as they advised our staff and leadership about making our congregation a safe, welcoming place for all people.

Congregational Life

I cannot begin to imagine how exhausting it was for Martha and Nick to educate everyone they encountered about communicating with their son. For every person who was kind and encouraging, there was another who was rude or cruel. A mother at their grade school said, "Kids like yours don't belong in public school. Put him some place where he belongs." A patron at the ballpark, fueled with beer courage, called Brad a demeaning name as he and his dad made their first appearance at a high school football game. A member of our parish, during the exchange of peace, whispered in Martha's ear, "It is such a tragedy about your son." (Nick and Martha almost left our church after that cruel comment. Trembling with anger, she told me, "Our son is not a tragedy.")

It was the practice of our congregation to commune all the baptized, welcoming children to the table as soon as they or their parents expressed an interest. Brad's little brother Joey, impatient with "only" a blessing at the communion table, started pestering his parents about getting the bread and wine. We started a conversation with Joey, providing education in the congregation and materials for his family to use at home. Martha and Nick invited me to their home for a meal, to talk over their table about the church's table. It turned out that Joey wasn't the only one interested in communion. Brad had begun signing the word for "bread" on Sunday mornings, also wanting to take greater part in the Lord's Supper.

We began to prepare in earnest for Brad's and Joey's first communion, practicing with them both, first at home and then in the sanctuary. I cannot recall how many times Martha and Brad came to church during the week when the sanctuary was empty, practicing the walk up the aisle, receiving the bread. We quickly learned that the cup of wine was too confusing, so we agreed that Brad would commune under only one element. We wanted to make sure there were no surprises for Brad when he received the Lord's Supper the first time.

None of us was prepared for what happened that day. Brad was beside himself with excitement, almost galloped up the aisle. (Joey was excited, too, but his excitement was not so publicly evident.) When we placed the bread in Brad's hands, spoke the familiar words "The body of Christ given for you" over his bobbing head, Brad plunged his nose into the bread. He smelled it for a long time, practically inhaling it, pressing it to the tip of his nose, finally consuming it with gusto. Brad's fascination with the bread never diminished; his delight in being part of our meal never grew old.

We Are Not Worthy

I came of age in the Lutheran church when first communion was withheld until after confirmation. We taught and believed that communion, unlike baptism, required understanding and knowledge, some effort on our part. I am not sure if my teenage classmates and I alternately slept and sweated through three years of Saturday morning confirmation class in order to receive the elusive Lord's Supper, be confirmed, or simply get it over with. I am certain we studied Holy Communion at some point, because I can still recite Luther's "What is Holy Communion?" from *The Small Catechism* word-for-word. But of its significance, its import, I was unaware. Confirmation and First Communion were often occasions for a new dress, a family party and no more Saturday morning classes. However, I do remember the parched communion wafer (dubbed "Christ Crispies" by an irreverent friend) on my tongue, trying desperately not to cough it up and thus diminish the power of the sacrament.

What did I know? I was fourteen-years-old, awkward and self-conscious. If understanding and knowledge were prerequisites for worthily receiving the Lord's Supper, I failed on both counts.

Our church body has taught that the grace and mercy extended in the sacraments are God's work and not ours, therefore age or education ought not be the sole prerequisite. Think about it. If baptism or communion were withheld until the recipient was able to cogently and accurately articulate the full meaning of the sacrament, there are few of us who would ever measure up. The baptismal font would be mothballed for lack of use, the bread baked in thimble-sized pans to accommodate the worthy few. Rather, we teach that God extends these gifts of grace to sinners before we are able to adequately receive them, trusting that we will grow into their meaning, into their significance, into that "love for us while we were yet sinners" (Rom 5:8) even as we grow in years. For that reason, it is now common in our churches to extend Holy Communion to all the baptized, offering a crumb of bread and a finger dipped in wine to even the smallest of infants, sometimes still wet from being washed in the font.

But it is not only the age of reception that provokes controversy among us. Brad's presence at our congregation's communion table was not universally appreciated. More than one person questioned his "worthiness" to receive the bread. After all, they argued, Brad didn't understand a single thing about the sacrament; he was simply imitating his parents' behavior. One scoffed, "A monkey would ask for the bread, too. Would you give it to him?" Sadly, their upset at welcoming a child with autism to our table is not unique. The question of "worthiness" is also raised about the public sinner, the forgetful elder, the cognitively disabled, the immigrant who stumbles with English. Is it "proper" for us to share the sacrament with those who are unable to understand or articulate their belief?

Martin Luther himself tossed and turned over the question of "worthiness," specifically, the worthiness or lack thereof of the priest who presides at the sacraments. A friend of mine received his first communion at the hands of a pastor later convicted of trafficking in child pornography. A congregation of my acquaintance communes only those who are known to the pastor or the council president, for fear of communing one who is "unworthy." I was once denied communion in a congregation I was visiting because the pastor did not believe women should be ordained—I was, to him, an unrepentant, unworthy sinner.

We are so afraid of either getting it wrong or doing it right that we fail to recognize the gift given so freely. It is the difference between a party host who makes all feel welcome, kindly overlooking the spilled wine or the wrong fork, and the host who demands perfect table manners and, in so doing, makes the meal a test rather than a gift.

When Luther wrote of the Sacrament of the Altar, he determined that three things are necessary for a practice to be sacramental:

1. The practice is commanded by Christ in scripture (see Matthew 28 for baptism and Matthew 26 for communion).

2. The practice includes a physical element (water in baptism, bread and wine in communion).

3. The practice conveys God's forgiving grace and mercy.

Luther also wrote, in regard to our ability to justify ourselves before God, "I believe that by my own understanding or strength I cannot believe in Jesus Christ my Lord or come to him."[1]

Similarly in scripture, when the Apostle Paul wrote to the Corinthian congregation about eating and drinking without discerning the body (1 Cor 11:27–34), he was not worried about the form of Christ's body laid in our hands or the question of our worthiness to receive it, but about our stubborn inability and unwillingness to recognize the living, breathing, sinning, starving body of Christ chewing and swallowing all around us.

Who is worthy?

---

1. Luther, "The Small Catechism" in *Evangelical Lutheran Worship*, 1162.

We Are Not Worthy

There are Sundays when it feels as though the pastor is called on to be waiter as well as presider, the long menu of table options requiring skilled interpretation. Wine or juice? Red or white? Whole wheat or gluten-free? Unleavened or yeast? Pouring chalice or intinction or common cup? Kneeling or standing? I overheard a disgruntled comment on an Easter Sunday as we invited worshippers to process for communion, stepping to one station to receive the bread, another station to receive the wine. "That's not communion," she sputtered. "It's a cattle call."

Even though, through years of practice, I have become skilled at negotiating the slalom gates erected between us and the Lord's Table, I am still occasionally surprised by special requests from guests at the meal.

Week after week Michael and his family, regular visitors in our parish, came forward for communion. Week after week, Michael's wife and children received the bread and wine, while he asked for only a blessing. I was left to guess at the reason for his unwillingness to receive the elements. Was he not baptized? Was he allergic to the bread or wine? Did the hand of blessing on his head convey more grace than the bread and wine? Did he have a physical ailment that precluded swallowing?

Over friendly conversation at his office, I learned Michael's reason for abstaining. Apparently, after a thorough reading of the New Testament and early church history, Michael was convinced that the only biblically faithful method of receiving the communion bread was in unleavened form. Since our congregation served whatever homemade bread our altar guild prepared that week, he did not consider leavened bread a valid expression of our Lord's intent, and thus, would not receive it. He asked me to provide unleavened bread for him so that he could commune with a clear conscience and in a biblical manner.

His argument was carefully reasoned.

I listened respectfully.

Then I refused.

We often make special arrangements for communion distribution, providing grape juice to a recovering alcoholic, honoring gluten-intolerance, taking the bread and wine into the pews to commune those unable to walk easily. We are not averse to accommodating special needs.

But Michael's concern was different. His concern was born not of need but of superior knowledge, deeper understanding, thinly veiled disdain for our misguided communion practice. I perceived his refusal to accept the offered bread as arrogance in the face of grace. Because of his insistence on receiving the Lord's Supper on his terms, he chose not to receive it at all.

There was no anger between us, no harsh words were spoken. But week after week he asked only for a blessing, refusing the yeasty body of Christ because it did not meet his standards.

One Sunday Michael approached the table with tear-filled eyes and outstretched hands. Hesitantly, I laid the pungent sourdough body of Christ into his moist palms. He buried his face in his hands, lingering over the bread, holding up the line, as he gently, thoughtfully, thoroughly consumed Jesus' body. He hugged me. I hugged him back. Michael drank deeply of the wine when it was offered, kissing the cup bearer on her cheek before returning to his seat. Only God knows how long it had been since Michael's last communion, but it was clear he was hungry for this, his first with us.

Michael later admitted that it was his son who had opened his eyes and heart, opened his hands. After yet another tedious Sunday Dinner Discussion with Dad about the error of serving leavened bread at communion, his grade-school son blurted, "Dad, do you refuse a present because you don't like the paper it's wrapped in? Dad, it's a gift. Just take it. Say 'thanks.'"

Often now on Sunday mornings, as I elevate the still-doughy-in-the-middle loaf of bread, slop the cheapest-red-wine-from-the-liquor-store on crisp white linens, I think about Michael and his wise young son. They are among that great cloud of witnesses assembled each week as we gather for worship. I remember them especially when I myself am torn about the Lord's Supper.

Each week we are called on to commune a motley crew of believers: the grieving widow, the yawning teenager, the wiggling toddler, the smug "I can last longer than any pastor" matriarch, the hormone-driven college students tangled around each other, the midlife couple whose marriage is strained to breaking, the old duffer so lonely he talks to himself, the respected businessman leading a not-so-respectable private life. Sometimes, when I am feeling small-minded or selfish, I hesitate before offering the bread, before extending the cup.

"Is he worthy? Is she worthy?" I ask myself.

However, it is not mine to question the sinner's desire for the meal, any more than it is mine to critique the form under which the meal is offered. I often return to the words of one of our Eucharistic prayers: "we give thanks to you not as we ought, but as we are able." Far from being who I ought to be, I do as I am able: tear the bread, extend the cup, offer the blessing.

We Are Not Worthy

To be honest, our denomination's communion practice is not as seamless as I have portrayed. There is great diversity and much disagreement among Lutherans about who and how and when. There is even more variety and tension with our brothers and sisters of other Christian faiths. We routinely erect barriers of worthiness or form between God and those who seek God's gift of grace.

Most of the time I am too occupied with the mundane details of daily parish ministry to pay much attention to the issue of communion practice. But when a young person visits a friend's non-Lutheran congregation, only to be turned away from the table, I am reminded of our disagreements. When a forgetful, frailing elder is no longer able to swallow the bread or wine, I grieve our fragility. And when, while planning a wedding or funeral, we debate the wisdom of offering the sacrament because it might divide rather than unite, I am saddened that this gift has become a problem to be solved.

Most of us will be under the sod or scattered to the wind before there is complete agreement about communion practice in Christ's church. But in this interim between Jesus' last supper with his disciples and our first communion in the kingdom of heaven, we carry on. We will be communed by clergy and laity of all kinds—exemplary citizens and accomplished sinners. We will receive the body of Christ in its many forms—bread burned or baked, leavened or flat, wine sparkling or sweet, red or white.

What makes a sacrament a sacrament is that it comes to us as a gift freely given by One who loves us beyond reason. The bread and wine and word laid in our hands and on our hearts become for us the body and blood of Christ, the Word of Life. This is God's gift, given to abject sinners. So whether this if our first communion or our last, it is pure gift. We need only receive it and say thanks.

Congregational Life

We Are Not Worthy Questions for Discussion

1. What is the central dilemma posed by this essay?

2. Describe the pattern and practices of Holy Communion in your faith community.

3. Who is eligible to commune in your faith community? Who gets to decide?

4. Who is excluded, either intentionally or unintentionally?

5. What is gained by welcoming all to participate in the Lord's Supper? What is lost?

Daily Life

15

Still Known

"We need a Lutheran pastor who knows something about babies." It was the hospital chaplain on the phone. Just moments before the call, a pregnant woman and her husband, Sandy and Neal, had arrived at the hospital, chauffeured by a neighbor from their home, a two hour's drive away. Early that morning she had gone into labor with their first child and, as previously arranged, the neighbor drove them to the hospital, while another was assigned to take care of the dogs in their absence. The infant car seat was already strapped into the neighbor's car, in anticipation of another, tiny passenger on the way home. But sometime between their phone call to their neighbor in the wee hours of the morning—"It's time"—and the car's arrival at the hospital, the child in her womb died. Sandy later said she knew something was wrong before they parked at the hospital. The child who had danced and punched inside her for months had grown oddly silent.

It was, sadly, no surprise then, when the admitting physician looked up at her after an initial exam: "I'm sorry. Something is wrong with your baby." As Lutherans far from home and without a local pastor, it was they who first asked for a Lutheran pastor.

My only point of reference was my own daughter's birth, one of the sweetest moments in my life. The pregnancy had been uneventful, the labor manageable, her birth in the dark hours of a frigid winter morning a quiet miracle. Naïvely, I imagined all births were as seamless and joyful.

When I stepped into the hospital room for what I imagined to be a brief visit, my illusions about childbirth (and the importance of my schedule) vanished as quickly as had the movement of the child in the womb. Sandy lay weeping in the hospital bed, her belly full of a child who would never breathe. Neal sat beside her, absently stroking her hand, staring out the window at the first light on the horizon. I am rarely at a loss for words, but at that moment there were none. I went to the other side of the bed, took Sandy's hand and said, "My name is JoAnn. I'm a Lutheran pastor. I'll stay as long as you need me."

I did stay, going home once to change clothes and to check on my family. Sandy's labor pains ebbed and flowed, sometimes intense, other times still. She slept intermittently. Her physician pressed her at the beginning of the second day: "Sandy, we need to get the baby out. This is going on too long." And as calmly as though it were a rehearsed line from a play she said, "No. When my baby is born, I will never be able to hold him again. I'm keeping him as long as I can." By sheer force of will, it seemed, she held her baby safely inside her through that second day.

During our two days together Sandy and Neal talked with me about their lives, their marriage, their pregnancy, about dreams dashed on the rocks. We talked about baptism. Because we had time to talk, and because they had no illusions about what lay ahead of them, I told them that since their child would be stillborn, there was no need to baptize, that their child would be born immediately into the arms of God. They accepted that explanation. We did, however, plan a Naming for their child. There would be ritual and laying on of hands and prayer at his birth. But no baptism.

Near the end of the second day, a change came over Sandy and she said, "It's time." The physician was called. Neal pulled back on one knee and I on the other to assist the delivery. Finally, with one mighty push and a burst of blood and water, their child was born. He was large and perfect and beautiful, his head covered with sticky white curls. And he was still as death, black as coal. Sandy turned her face into her pillow and reached between her legs to touch his steaming warm head, too tired to speak or to cry. Neal looked down on his firstborn son, wrapped an infant finger around his own and began to howl. Like an animal, the anger and pain, the fear and disappointment of the last two days poured out of his mouth in a fierce and piercing moan. He ran into the hallway and collapsed there on the floor. The physician sat slumped in a corner, huge tears rolling down her face. (Later she told me that she was going to stop delivering babies. She and her husband were trying to get pregnant and she simply couldn't bear the sorrow anymore.) I just stood there, standing silent guard until Neal could return and Sandy could speak.

Still Known

Their first child received his name. Joseph. The name they had chosen months before. Sandy held Joseph; Neal held her. The physician served as our congregation. We read from Isaiah 43, "Do not fear, for I have redeemed you; I have called you by name." And from Psalm 139, "Before I formed you in the womb I knew you." Laying trembling hands on his already-cooling head, I cradled those beautiful curls and said, "We name you Joseph, the name by which you will be known on earth and in heaven." The naming was sealed with an oily cross on his forehead. Sandy and Neal then baptized him with their tears.

They remained in the city with family members, to heal and for the funeral. After they had returned to their home, I had time to reflect on what had happened. With no warning, with no training, guided only by parental love and God's mercy, Sandy's labor and Neal's care, Joseph's birth was perfect. If there is a "right" way to deliver a stillborn child, they did it. From a pastoral standpoint, I trust that I cared for them well, serving as midwife and pastor, sister and friend to these strangers in need.

I thought of them and prayed for them often. I cherished their trust. As naïvely as I had imagined all births to be like my daughter's I imagined that all stillbirths could be so carefully controlled, so gently tended. But it was also an experience I never needed to have again.

Many years later, I received a similarly anxious phone call from a different hospital about a different family in trouble. "We need you now. The baby came too soon." But this time I knew the family in need, had celebrated their pregnancy. I grabbed my purse-sized Bible, threw on a coat and rushed to the hospital, hoping that "too soon" did not mean what I feared it might.

Emily had gone into labor weeks too early. Emily and Scott had barely made it to the hospital before their son forced his way into the world. The baby never drew a breath, never uttered a cry. He was dead before he had had a chance to live.

As I raced into the hospital, a nurse who also happened to be a member of our congregation was waiting for me at the door. "Slow down. It's over. There is no rush." I took a deep cleansing breath. She quietly escorted me to Emily's room, parted the curtain beside the bed and led me in. Emily looked up at me from the bed with empty eyes, her husband, Scott, ashen, kneeling beside her as once he had knelt to propose. Their infant son was already bathed and dressed, swaddled in a hospital blanket because Grandma had not yet finished the blanket in which they planned to bring him home.

Without preamble, her voice void of emotion, Emily said, "His name is William. We want him baptized." Without reflection or protest, I said, "Of course." The nurse found a basin of water and a towel. A makeshift congregation gathered around the bed—nursing staff, physician, grandparents. We baptized a dead child in the name of the triune God.

When William was duly baptized, Emily turned her head and said to all of us, "Leave now." We left Emily and Scott to say good-bye to William without an audience.

Our time together had lasted only minutes. Their need was so raw, their request so simple. It took me a long time to process what had happened. Lutherans do not baptize the dead because the dead do not need to be baptized. A stillborn child belongs to God long before we ever see his face, and baptism for those already held in God's arms is simply not necessary. I knew all that, taught all that, believed all that. I have always prided myself on doing the right thing, even if it was hard.

But all that certainty had faded with a physically exhausted, grieving mother's request to baptize her stillborn child. The "right" way no longer mattered. Her need for that familiar sign far outweighed any principles I held. Her need for assurance that her William belonged completely and wholly to God trumped any careful explanation of sacramental theology I could have offered at the time. Unlike that incredibly teachable moment with Sandy and Nick years before, this was no teachable moment. Their need was immediate and stark. Baptism was the only thing that would satisfy.

I had been ordained only a few years when I attended Joseph's birth. I portrayed a pastoral confidence I did not feel; presented pastoral skills I did not own. Yet somehow, in spite of my lack of experience and trembling knees, I knew what to do. Neal and Sandy showed me; God guided me; the physician coached me. If there is a "right" way to assist a stillbirth, it was realized with that small family.

So why did I not do the "right" thing with Scott and Emily? Why did I consent to a ritual that was, theologically speaking, unnecessary? Certainly, no harm was done. But is the lack of harmful consequence justification for such an action?

Still Known

I have come under criticism from colleagues with whom I have shared these two stories. It is clear that not every pastor would have responded as I did. Some would have baptized Joseph without hesitation. Some would have refused baptism to William. Some have argued that regardless what path I chose, I should have been consistent.

I have come to learn that "doing the right thing" is an elusive and sometimes pointless goal. I remain convinced of the power of Lutheran sacramental theology. I marvel at the depth of scriptural wisdom about God's mercy, even for the dead. I cherish the restraint and dignity of Lutheran worship and prayer. Guided by all that—theology, scripture, tradition—I know that the "right" thing must also be tempered by the pastoral thing. Steeped in scripture, theology, and tradition, well-loved and firmly guided, I have a deep pastoral sense of what to do next—whether that decision is made in a hospital room or at a kitchen table or in the church parking lot after a meeting. Whether I have two days to make a decision, or two minutes.

During three decades of parish ministry, I have made countless mistakes in judgment. I say things I ought not say. I miss cues. I let the immediate crowd out the necessary. I imagine I will need another thirty years simply to figure out how to pastor well, to ask forgiveness for my daily miscalculations and lapses in judgment.

Yet there are moments when pastoral wisdom blossoms, when even I am surprised at the gracious word that escapes my mouth, the tender touch in my hand, the unplanned clarity that opens a way.

I know that both Joseph and William are fully in God's care and keeping—from before they were born until we see them again. And I know that Neal and Sandy, now the parents of two living boys, remember Joseph's birth with gratitude and peace. I know that Scott and Emily, now parents of a daughter, have taken enormous comfort in William's baptism.

I am humbled by my participation in those remarkable, heartbreaking births. I am grateful for finding the right words when they were necessary, for silence when it was healing, for simple actions that eased their pain. I know I was a pastor to them when a pastor was what they needed. I marvel again, at the wisdom of God—so much greater than my own—that made the "right" thing out of births that went so wrong. And though stillborn, both these children, all our children, are still known to God.

Daily Life

Still Known Questions for Discussion

1. What is the central dilemma posed by this essay?

2. When doctrinal or theological issues and pastoral care needs are in tension, how does one determine the most faithful course of action? Is there a "right" way?

3. In each case, what was at stake in the pastor's decision?

4. Does the desire to comfort and console trump other pastoral considerations?

16

Not a Prayer

"A Methodist, a Lutheran, a Disciple of Christ, a Roman Catholic, a Congregationalist and a Presbyterian walk into a bar."

This could be the opening of a stale tavern joke, or a description of our local clergy group. Most often, such colleague groups are gatherings of the like-minded and denominationally affiliated, but we were able, for a short time, to bring together clergy from across the Christian theological spectrum. Our primary purpose was to engage in fellowship and to share work on community projects. We also drank together—coffee in a church basement.

One thing we did not do was pray together. Some of our colleagues would not pray with clergy of other denominations for fear of seeming to be in agreement with them. It was awkward to be in a room full of Christians for whom prayer was anathema. But we soldiered on, usually without a prayer.

One cold January, as the annual Week of Prayer for Christian Unity approached, one of our colleagues proposed a radical project. What if, for one year, each of our congregations prayed for another congregation in our city each Sunday? In the course of a year, we would have prayed for all of our congregations twice. It seemed a brilliant way for us to pray together, without actually being in the same room or violating denominational sensitivities.

It took some time to hammer out the details and the order in which we would assign the congregations for prayer. We finally worked out a plan that respected our differences and supported one another's ministries at the same time.

Daily Life

Just as the discussion was coming to a close, as we pushed chairs away from the table and gathered coffee cups for washing, one of our brothers cleared his throat to get our attention. He had one more question: "Do the prayers have to be *nice*?"

Praying shouldn't be that hard, should it? But it is. In many cases, prayer has become freighted with religious and political baggage, the prayers of one seen as rebuke of another. When we pray, are we trying to impress those who are watching and hearing our prayers? (See "And when you pray . . ." in Matthew 6). Or is it enough *that* we pray, that God hears us, whether we pray in public or in the privacy of our own rooms? And what do we hope to accomplish in prayer? Arm-twisting? Begging? Reminding? Resigning?

It may surprise some to learn that a professional petitioner like me struggles with these questions. After all, I get paid to pray. It's my job. I've prayed in gymnasiums and synagogues and prisons, at graveside and bedside, business lunches and ladies' circles. I've prayed for fire fighters and police officers, funeral directors and felons. My prayers have been applauded. Once, I'm ashamed to say, I prayed for a dead dog, clutching its collar along with Fido's grieving owners. "We just want to make sure he's in heaven when we get there," they pleaded. I hope God wasn't listening.

You would think that, after all these years, I would know what I was doing. And why. But I have never been clear about why we pray, or how best to pray. I have always struggled with the notion of "prayer chains," multiplying the number of prayers catapulted heavenward. Do more prayers produce better outcomes? And, if God knows all our needs, why pester God with additional information? I have worried that my prayers are little more than gnats buzzing around God's ears.

Additionally, is there a difference between praying for specific outcomes for specific people (a friend's illness, an upcoming job interview) and praying about the Big Things—world peace, homelessness and hunger, violence and devastation? If I pray healing for a friend who dies anyway, what good were my prayers? If we're all praying for peace, why do wars keep popping up? Why pray if nothing comes of it?

Why we pray. How we pray. When and where we pray. To whom we address petitions. Who gets to pray. These issues have long festered in my heart. Yet, while they fester, I keep on praying. Sometimes, secretly, I find myself praying that I might have a prayer, words worthy of God's attention

Not a Prayer

and the plight of those for whom I pray, because there are times when I haven't got one. It is then that I lean on the Apostle Paul's description of prayer as "sighs too deep for words." (Rom 8:26) There might be times when I cannot pray, but I can sigh with the best of them.

There was a long stretch of time one winter when I was on disability leave from the parish while undergoing chemotherapy. It was a grim time in every respect. The diagnosis of cancer had knocked me off my feet. The treatments were brutal, the side effects debilitating, bad enough at times that I begged them to stop and just let me die. I felt myself a failure as wife and mother, friend and neighbor during those months. My poor dogs languished without their long walks. In addition to those cancer-common hardships, I missed my parish immensely. To be parted from people I knew and loved at one of the darkest times of my life seemed an unreasonable and harsh burden.

Even though I could not attend to them, they attended tirelessly to us. My family and I were inundated with food and flowers, cards and love. Congregations and friends all over the world prayed for us. Colleagues visited. The children of our congregation's nursery school wrote a book for me. Muslim friends remembered me before the Beloved. A rabbinical friend sang Hebrew psalms to me during a treatment. My enormous extended family loved us from afar. With every card that came in the mail, every message on my blog, every meal that warmed our bellies, every visit in our home, came these words, "We are praying for you."

What were they praying for? Did it make a difference in my healing that thousands were praying for me? Did those ceaseless petitions make a difference to God? I can't know. But they did make a difference to me.

One particularly pathetic January morning, as side effects from chemotherapy messed with my body and my mind, I was moping around the house—depressed, discouraged, depleted. And then the phone rang. I almost didn't answer it. Most daytime phone calls were from telemarketers, and I wasn't in the mood for a sales pitch about siding and windows. The caller identified herself as Pastor Samson, leader of a local Pentecostal church. "I have a burden on my heart for you. I've called to pray with you."

"On the phone?" I asked.

"Yes. On the phone. Now."

So we prayed.

Daily Life

I have prayed with people on the phone before, but it is not my preferred method. But Pastor Samson is a woman of profound faith and significant personal power, a woman not easily deterred. She quickly drew me into her outstretched AT&T arms and began to pray, almost to preach. It was clear she and God were on a first name basis, that she had bent God's ear about me before; no introductions were needed. She launched into a litany of requests: healing, courage, strength, protection, peace. She prayed for my husband and daughters by name. Her bids were respectful, but urgent—God was not going to get away easily. Her voice rose and her words tumbled over one another. It was hard for me to keep up, but it was God who had to pay attention. I was just along for the ride.

I had never been prayed for so directly, so forcefully. I had to sit down.

After detailing her expectations to God, she turned her attention to the Devil, who had been (metaphorically speaking) tiptoeing his sorry behind out the door and out of her reach. For Pastor Samson, the devil was real, tangible, a tiresome troublemaker needing constant supervision. She grabbed him by the scruff of the neck, rebuked and mocked and tossed him aside. "You have no power here!" she shouted simultaneously in God's ear and mine.

And then she praised. We praised. "Thank you. Thank you. Thank you." Six, seven, eight times. I lost count. I had collapsed, exhausted, on the bottom step of our oak staircase, clutching the phone to my ear, tears streaming down my face. "Thank you. Thank you," she cried. And finally, "Praise the Lord! Amen!"

Then we were done.

"I'll keep praying for you," she promised. "God's richest blessings to you and your family." Click.

Pastor Samson's presence across the airwaves was as powerful as if she had been in the room with me, as if her strong hands had been pressed on my bowed head, her brown eyes boring into my soul, her mighty faith wrapped around me like a cloak. I was a sweaty mess when I put down the phone. I'm guessing God had to sit for a minute, too. We'd both had a workout.

I was grateful for and humbled by her prayer and by the legion of others whose prayers carried us in those months. But I didn't know what to make of it.

Not a Prayer

Since that dark time of treatment and its enforced isolation from community, I have had time to reflect on Pastor Samson's prayer, and the thousands of petitions thrown God's way on my behalf. People all over the world prayed for healing, for comfort, for peace. Some even prayed for a miracle. And how were those prayers answered? After nine months of surgery, testing, and chemotherapy, I did go back to my "old life" of pastoring and dog walking and traveling and tasting food, rather than just feeling it. Though I am now cancer-free, I'm living with a cancer that may easily rear its head again one day. My oncologist said, "Think about your cancer like diabetes or heart disease. You'll be in treatment or testing for the rest of your life."

So was I healed? Comforted? Am I at peace? Was I the recipient of a miracle? Did all those prayers "work"?

Even as I write those questions, I know that they are off-base, not the point at all. Here's my current thinking on the subject: the point of prayer is that we pray. It is not to manipulate God to see it our way, or that God's mind is changed, or the course of history altered. The point of the prayer is the praying itself.

I imagine that prayer is about being so deeply in relationship with God and God's people that we are in constant conversation with and about them. We can talk to God about anything. Big things. Small things. Petty fears and passionate wishes. It doesn't matter what we say. God hears it all.

Old Testament scholar Walter Brueggemann once told a class I attended that "anything that can be said, can be said to God."

A friend who lives far from her parents is on the phone with her mother and sisters daily. I asked her once if they ever run out of things to talk about. She said, "Nope. The more we talk, the more we have to talk about."

"Talk to me," the loving parents begs the silent child. "Just talk to me. Whatever it is, we'll face it together."

So it is with prayer.

God's will *will* be done regardless of my begging and pleading, but, as Martin Luther writes:

> God wants to attract us, so that we come to believe God is truly our Father and we are truly God's children, in order that we may ask God boldly and with complete confidence, just as loving children ask their loving Father.[1]

---

1. Luther, "The Small Catechism," in *Evangelical Lutheran Worship*, 1163.

Daily Life

∞

The congregation I served was bursting at the seams with children and activity and community use. While lovely, the building was better suited to ministry in the nineteenth rather than the twenty-first century. Previous pastors had toyed with the idea of doing something with the building, but soon discovered that retrofitting a one-hundred-year-old facility was daunting, if not impossible. However, the longer I served there, the more apparent it became that the building was holding us back.

Pastor Pennington, one of the members of the aforementioned clergy group, served a neighboring congregation that had just completed a major renovation and rebuild of their facility. While the memory of that project was fresh in his memory, I wanted to pick his brain, pose my questions to him. How did you decide to build? What was your process? Who informed you along the way? How did you pay for it? What would you do differently?

Pastor Pennington and I had never been close. Besides the differences between the denominations we served, he and I didn't like each other much. There was no open warfare, but we did not choose to associate in anything but public settings.

However, it seemed shortsighted and small of me to ignore his wisdom simply because we were not BFF's. He responded favorably to my request to talk, even invited me to his office for the conversation. I went to our meeting armed with a notepad full of questions and ideas. He was patient with me, willing to share both the triumphs and the failures of their building project. The meeting was cool, but cordial. In the back of my mind, I wondered if, more than pondering a common problem, perhaps we were making first steps toward a better working relationship.

My wondering was quickly derailed when, at the end of our conversation, he asked if we could pray together. I was surprised—he was one of the colleagues who would not pray with our clergy group—but pleased. Who wouldn't want to invoke God's blessing, wisdom and guidance on the threshold of a new venture?

We bowed our heads, and he began to pray:

"O God, you know that JoAnn can be impulsive and misguided. You know that she has aspirations greater than she ought, that she is not up to the task she proposes. She is young and foolish—."

Are your surprised that I can quote his prayer verbatim after all these years? I was flabbergasted and angry. What happened to the collegial conversation we had just enjoyed? This was not prayer, but an attack. It was sheer cowardice—criticism couched as conversation with the Almighty. To tell you the truth, I do not remember what followed the part about "young and foolish." After his "Amen," which I did not echo, I clumsily gathered my things and stumbled to the door. Just the thought of it, years later, makes my blood boil.

Pastor Pennington pretended that he was praying for me. But he did not have a prayer; he had an agenda. Prayer is addressed to God, not the person for whom we pray. Nor is prayer an excuse to say what you really think under the guise of piety. In fact, he was the colleague who had asked if prayers for one another's congregations had to be "nice."

I have mulled that moment for years now, and have yet to find peace. Even if what Pastor Pennington said was true, that I can be impulsive and foolish, prayer was not the place for that assessment.

To be fair to Pastor Pennington, he can say anything he wants to God. As can I. That he did not care for or respect me is certainly his prerogative. But in his "prayer" he was not praying that God's will would be done in my life or the life of my congregation, but that his will would be imposed on me. I am not above correction or advice, so if his concerns for me were valid, they should have been raised in conversation, not under the guise of prayer.

The contrast between Pastor Pennington's damning indictment of my faults, and Pastor Samson's direct address to God on my behalf could not be more stark. He was judgmental and harsh; she was direct and hopeful. He demonstrated cowardice; she was living, breathing courage.

Why do we pray? What do we pray? To whom do we address our bids? What do we hope to accomplish? Sometimes I actually take those questions up with God. Because questions can be prayers, too.

So, even though I'm not always sure why I do it, I keep praying. I pray for the sick and the well, the living and the dying. I pray for peace in the world and for heating fuel in a particular home. I pray for Congress and for criminals. I pray for my enemies and those who love me more than they should. And sometimes I just sit in God's presence, completely out of words to either plead or praise. Because I know God is listening, even when I haven't got a prayer.

Daily Life

Not a Prayer Discussion Questions

1. What is the central dilemma posed by this essay?

2. What motivates you to pray?

3. What do you pray for?

4. What do you hope might happen when you pray?

5. What image describes your understanding of prayer? Conversation? Begging? Instructing? Unburdening? Sharing? Something else?

17

Marry Me?

Why do we wed? It seems an odd question, since the answer is so obvious. Clearly, we marry for love. Don't we?

In fact, many do marry for love, having found a person who makes their heart sing, whose presence lights a dark room, whose touch ignites fireworks every time, who draws from us our very best.

But that has not been and is not always the case.

In previous generations, the promise to "be faithful until death parts us," was a more time-sensitive matter than it is today. Life expectancy was shorter. Simple illnesses could kill. Women often died in childbirth. Rarely did couples celebrate a fiftieth wedding anniversary—they didn't live that long. "Until death parts us" was serious business.

In addition, love was not the primary reason our ancestors wed. Sometimes marriage was a purely practical matter. They married because unmarried daughters were expensive to keep, and because sons needed help with the family business. They married to legitimize a sexual relationship. They married to provide a stable environment for child-rearing. They married because it was to each family's advantage, either socially or financially. They married because a young widow or widower with children couldn't manage alone. They married to assuage loneliness.

Though love was not the primary reason for marrying, it often grew.

But now, in our time and in our culture, those practical reasons for marriage often simply don't apply. Women and men are able to support themselves financially without need of a spouse. Sexual relationships before marriage are common and are no longer hidden. Children can be born or adopted into any number of family models. Loneliness can be managed through relationships other than marriage. Among older people, marriage can complicate pensions and retirement plans, making marriage a financially unwieldy proposition. In fact, marriage rates are dropping each decade as fewer and fewer people regard marriage as either a necessary or a desirable thing.

So, the question remains. Why do we marry?

Marcia had been happily married to her high school sweetheart for ten years. They shared the parenting of two small children. He worked long hours for the Department of Transportation on a road crew, amassing as much overtime as he could so that Marcia could stay at home and raise their family. They had the life of which they had dreamed.

With one icy skid on a winter road, a car wrapped around a telephone pole, and their dream became a nightmare. Overnight, Marcia went from being a happy stay-at-home mom to being a widowed single mother with two grade-school children, no marketable skills, no health insurance, and a crippling burden of grief. Her parents lived nearby and were able to carry much of the load. On days when Marcia could not lift herself from bed, they would put the children on the school bus, get Marcia up and dressed and fed. They kept house for her, paid bills for her, supported her until she could stand again. Our congregation stood by and supported her as well.

Gradually, Marcia resumed her life. Gradually, she became involved in the school and community and church and work and night classes. Gradually, she even learned to laugh again; after all, her son had his father's smile, her daughter twitched in her sleep the way her dad had. I was deeply impressed with Marcia's courage and strength, her hard-fought ability to rebuild a life shattered by her husband's unexpected and untimely death.

But one thing was missing. Marcia was tremendously lonely. Marcia had never lived alone, and she didn't like it. Though she was busy with work and studies and church choir and soccer games and school plays, none of those activities filled the hole in her heart, the empty place in the bed beside her.

Dating was far more difficult than she imagined.

"I hate being out on the market again," she groaned. "I feel like fresh meat." Married men made advances. Online dates were a bust. The one blind date to which she consented was tedious. "Isn't there anybody out there who is normal?"

At a high school class reunion she re-met a classmate she hadn't seen in fifteen years. He was recently divorced, seemed normal enough. Neither was ready for serious commitment, but they enjoyed one another's company and slowly eased into a relationship.

I was a little surprised when Marcia confided that her new beau had proposed marriage. Her boyfriend often came to church with her, so I knew him a bit. But I never felt the spark of passion between them that I had always sensed between Marcia and her first husband. Of course, what do I know of second marriages, of falling in love again? There are lots of ways to be in love, lots of ways to be married, so we began our wedding plans with great joy and hope.

It was a small wedding in a side chapel at our church. We sang and prayed. They made promises and exchanged rings. There were lots of tears, of joy and of sorrow. At a family dinner afterward, I kissed Marcia on the cheek and whispered, "I'm so happy for you." She whispered, "Me, too. Now the children have health insurance."

You could have knocked me over with a garter belt.

I know that, given the current state of affairs in this country, health insurance is not enjoyed by everyone, that it is a commodity to be protected and cherished. I cannot imagine the fear that kept Marcia awake at night, worrying what would happen if she or one of the children were injured or became gravely ill, and all they had for protection was the state-run insurance plan. But I never imagined the need for health insurance would drive a woman to the altar.

Perhaps Marcia did marry for love. Perhaps her new husband did bring her joy. Perhaps the additional benefit of health insurance for the children was just that—an additional benefit. But I always wondered if I had been duped into presiding at her wedding, if Marcia had married under false pretenses. My wondering was rekindled when the marriage was short-lived. He tired of her children. She tired of him. But by the time the marriage ended she had found work that offered both health insurance and retirement benefits, so the financial need for marriage was not so acute.

Why do we marry? The answer is not so clear.

I am very particular about presiding at weddings in the congregations I serve. My checklist before agreeing to preside includes things like:

Are they practicing Christians?

Are they members of or connected to the congregation?

Is there ample time to prepare for the celebration?

Is there reason to believe this relationship will last?

Perhaps the very presence of a checklist startles you. Shouldn't pastors delight to do weddings, to support love, to say yes to the dress and all that accompanies it? To be honest, from the pastor's perspective, weddings are more bane than blessing, not as romantic as one might imagine. From a pastor's point of view, the wedding is not nearly as important as the marriage. Focusing on the wedding rather than the years-long commitment of marriage is like putting fancy icing on a cardboard box—it looks pretty, but there's nothing there.

Ideally, wedding preparation is an opportunity for the couple to deepen their relationship with one another. We discuss marriage—the myths and the fact of it. We name the couple's hopes and fears. We take time to plan a liturgy, to select scripture texts and music, to involve friends and family in an event that not only celebrates the gift of marriage, but also stands as witness to God's intention for us.

We name that intention at the very beginning of the wedding liturgy:

> The scriptures teach us that the bond and covenant of marriage is a gift of God in which two are joined as one, an image of the union of Christ and the church.[1]

Marriage is a gift. Marriage is a holy union. Marriage is an image of God. When those things are clear and present, weddings are a delight to the couple and all who witness their vows, including the pastor.

Too often, however, weddings have little to do with shared faith or common witness or gratitude for God's gifts. Weddings are occasions to spend beyond our means, to indulge in fantasies fueled by the multi-billion-dollar-a-year wedding industry, to throw a party marked by excessive eating, drinking, dancing, and misbehaving.

Too often, couples worry more about the song list for the dance than the readings at the wedding. They complain about the organist's fees, but think nothing of spending thousands of dollars on party favors. The liturgy is truncated because the wedding planner has allotted only thirty minutes for the ceremony. Couples will promise anything to get a church wedding,

---

1. "Marriage" *Evangelical Lutheran Worship Leader's Edition*, 676.

Marry Me?

even if they have to lie to do it. A couple once admitted to me that they were marrying only because they had been living together so long, it was the only way to stop their parents' pestering.

It is a privilege to be part of the weddings of those who choose to marry in the church because the church is their home. It is an honor to witness the vows of those who build their marriage on faith in Jesus Christ. I do not hesitate to preside at such weddings. But when non-believers or photo-seekers request a church wedding because the building is pretty or the bride always wanted to walk down a long aisle or somebody's grandma will pay for the wedding only if it happens in a church, I balk.

"Until death parts us" is a serious matter.

I had met Marty and Beth on several social occasions, but had no other relationship with them. They were merely friends of friends, people I recognized at cocktail parties and at the grocery store. I knew bits and pieces of their story, that they had been together, though not married, for almost twenty years, were both employed by the state, that they were parents of three teenage children. I knew that they were not practitioners of any faith.

The friend who had first introduced us called one hot July morning to tell me that Marty had suffered a stroke and was hospitalized in critical condition. She asked if I would visit him. Her phone call had not prepared me for what I found. The stroke had been severe, leaving Marty paralyzed on one side of his body, hooked up to a tangle of tubes and monitors. Beth sat at his bedside, pale and exhausted.

Though we barely knew one another, they recognized me the moment I walked into the room. (A clerical collar often jogs the memory.) Marty started to cry when he saw me, tears running down his stroke-slackened cheek. Beth clung to me like a sailor to the mast of a sinking ship. "You came," she sobbed. "We hoped you would."

Still reeling from the shock of a stroke in a healthy man, not yet fifty years old, Beth related recent events. Marty, his speech slurred, added to her narrative as she went along. Though his condition was serious, they were hopeful that Marty would recover and eventually come home.

We sat silently for a time, Marty drifting off to sleep, Beth staring out the window. After a quiet interval she turned to me. "We've been meaning to call you for a long time, but never got around to it. We were wondering if you would marry us."

It was my turn to stare out the window, to collect my thoughts. I reviewed my wedding checklist quickly in my head. They did not fit any of my typical wedding criteria, but, rather than reflexively refuse her request, I asked Beth to tell me more.

Clearly, their desire to marry was spurred by the sudden change in Marty's health. "We always wanted to marry, but never found time," Beth admitted. "We were so stupid. Now we know that time is short and we don't want to wait any more."

Slowly, stumbling over his thick tongue, Marty confirmed what Beth said. "I've loved her since fifth grade," he said. "I should have married her then."

Beth leaned over the bed rail and buried her face in Marty's chest. They cried. I stewed.

"Go ahead and get a license," I said. "It would be an honor to preside at your wedding."

Three days later we gathered for the ceremony in the intensive care unit of the hospital. The staff dressed Marty in a fresh hospital gown. Beth had been home long enough to shower and brush her teeth, to put on a clean T-shirt and jeans. Their three rangy teenagers skipped school for the wedding. The charge nurse smuggled in a bouquet of flowers, saying, "It's against policy to have flowers on the unit, so I'll have to take them back when the wedding is over." Because hospital administrators were a bit nervous about the upcoming nuptials, the attending physician had to certify that Marty was of sound mind, and was not being coerced or persuaded.

In spite of all the gyrations and gymnastics, theirs was a wedding like all others—prayers, promises, rings. But when Marty slurred his vows, one side of his face sagging, I heard those familiar words as though for the first time. "I take you to be my wife, to join with you and share all that is to come. And I promise to be faithful to you until death parts us."

Only God knew how short that time would be.

Because of my earlier experience with Marcia, the cynic in me wondered if there might be other motives for marrying them so suddenly. I did not doubt that Beth and Marty had always intended to marry, and from a practical standpoint, it was wise. I knew that marriage would protect Beth financially and legally in the event of Marty's death. I knew that Beth could have been denied the right to make decisions with regard to Marty's health care, since they were not legally wed. There were more than enough pragmatic reasons for them to marry.

Marry Me?

But I was moved by their circumstance, touched by their honesty, swept up in their desire for the strong and hopeful sign of marriage in the midst of their unexpected sorrow.

Sadly, their promises to be married "until death parts us" were abruptly ended. Marty died that night, felled by a burst blood vessel in his brain about which nothing could be done.

Why do we wed?

Some of us marry for love—swept off our feet, unable to imagine life without the other.

Others of us marry for necessity—living alone is unacceptable to us.

Still others marry because it is the "next thing," or because they always wanted a wedding, or because an unplanned pregnancy changes minds, or for some other not-easily-articulated or readily admitted reason.

I do not criticize any of these reasons. None of us marries for a single, noble purpose. In fact, I have seen marriages survive and even thrive when begun under the most difficult—or the sketchiest—of circumstances.

My concern is not that people choose to marry. My concern is that when couples come to the church to marry, when they seek the services of a pastor and the presence of a community of faith, that they intend to honor their vows as the church articulates them.

When those who marry understand the reason for Christian marriage, these words which launch the marriage rite are cause for celebration:

> We have come together in the presence of God to witness the marriage of name and name, to surround them with our prayers, and to share in their joy.[2]

Why do we wed? Among Christians, this is the answer. We marry to witness, to pray, to share joy.

Later in the liturgy, the pastor announces:

> Name and name, by their promises before God and in presence of this assembly, have bound themselves to one another as husband and wife. Those whom God has joined together, let no one separate.[3]

---

2. "Marriage," *Evangelical Lutheran Worship Leader's Edition*, 676.
3. "Marriage," *Evangelical Lutheran Worship Pew Edition*, 288.

Daily Life

Under these circumstances, with this shared sense of God's presence in our vows, the assembly responds without hesitation and with a joyful shout: "Amen. Thanks be to God!"

Marry Me? Questions for discussion

1. What is the central dilemma posed by this essay?

2. Discuss the premise that those who wed in a church should have some relationship to the congregation.

3. Does a congregation have responsibility to those who wed in its building? Might they have expectations of the couple?

4. What is the difference between a marriage and a wedding?

18

Sincerely Dead

When I was a kid, *The Wizard of Oz* aired on our local television station once a year. That was back in the dark ages, when telephones were tethered to the wall, and "face book" was two words, and televisions had ears—rabbit ears, wrapped in foil. In those days, there were only three channels to choose from, but we were of necessity a CBS family—it was the only station our TV's rooftop antenna could detect.

The Wizard of Oz was an event at our house. Mom popped endless bowls of popcorn. The phone went unanswered. We sat glued to the television, tearing ourselves away only to use the bathroom or to hide behind the couch when the Wicked Witch's winged monkeys swooped down on a terrified Toto.

It is a feast of a film. Munchkins and Ozmites. Lions and tigers and bears, oh my. Ruby slippers. The Emerald City. Talking trees and narcotic poppies and the Horse of a Different Color. And this clever lyric, sung upon the discovery of the crushed-by-a-house Wicked Witch of the East:

> (She) is morally, ethic'lly, spiritually, physically,
> Positively, absolutely, undeniably and reliably Dead.
> As Coroner I must aver, I thoroughly examined her.
> And she's not only merely dead, she's really most sincerely dead.[1]

Sincerely dead. That's serious. And very final.

It seems, however, that only Munchkins believe death is absolute, undeniable, reliable and most sincere. Most of the language we use about death is a little less certain. We "pass on" or "pass over." We "expire." We

---

1. E. Y. "Yip" Harburg, "Ding, Dong, the Witch Is Dead," *The Wizard of Oz*.

Sincerely Dead

"leave this earth." We "go to a better place." We "fall asleep." Rarely, it seems, do we admit that we positively, absolutely, undeniably, reliably and most sincerely die.

But we do. We do die. And that fact seems to be a problem for many of us. Even for Christians.

Lisa was abandoned in stages. Shortly after her birth, her father was convicted of armed robbery, spending most of her childhood years in prison. Her mother found more comfort cradling a bottle of Southern Comfort than her baby. Her parents were in and out of Lisa's life for years, though mostly out. And when they were in, it was ugly.

It was Lisa's grandmother who provided stability and a home, her grandmother who loved and provided for her, her grandmother who served as both mother and father. But even though she was doted on by her grandmother and a gaggle of aunts, uncles and cousins, Lisa never was never able to make peace with her parents' chosen absence, the deep sense that she was worthless, that no one loved her best.

When Lisa married and had children, she struggled with what it meant to be a mother. She suffered massive postpartum depression, turned on her loving but befuddled husband. Once she walked away from the house, was gone for hours without explanation. Again, it was her grandmother who stepped in to provide stability and safety—for Lisa and her young family.

When Lisa's grandmother died unexpectedly, the lights went out in Lisa's heart. She sobbed uncontrollably through the wake and funeral, unable even to speak. Afterward she descended into a silent depression; no one could reach her.

Lisa became obsessed with a television psychic who claimed to communicate with the dead (for a fee). Lisa bought all the DVDs and books, sent money to the psychic for a personal consultation. The psychic claimed that the dead are not really dead. They are "in a better place." They are "waiting for us." They are "watching over us." The psychic promised Lisa that her grandmother would come back to her, would communicate with her. After all, when someone truly loves us, the psychic said, they would never leave us, they would never really die.

Lisa's reliance on a psychic might seem a bit extreme, but many who grieve report having had contact with the deceased. They have felt the loved one touch their cheek. Mom's favorite song comes on the radio on the anniversary of her death. The flower that Grandpa planted blooms out of season. I do not know what to make of these experiences, cannot attest to their validity. But I know that it happens often enough that some have come to regard it as normal, even expected.

Months after her grandmother's death, Lisa appeared unannounced at my office door. Almost too distraught to speak, she collapsed into a chair. Through her gulping sobs, I deciphered, "She hasn't come yet. Where is she? She never loved me. If she loved me, she would come."

It took a while for me to understand that Lisa was completely convinced her grandmother wasn't really dead, but just "in a better place" just outside her field of vision, just over the next rise. Lisa believed her grandmother would come to her, as the psychic had promised. In a dream, perhaps. In a vision. In a familiar whiff of perfume. In a gentle touch on her face.

"Why hasn't she come back? They promised me she would. Where is she?"

As gently as I could, I pried Lisa's hands from her face and held them tightly in my own. I looked her in the eye and said softly but firmly, "Lisa, your grandmother is dead. She won't be coming back."

We do no favors when we minimize the fact of death. Death is very final. And most sincere.

In the beginning, shortly after God created the heavens and the earth, the seas and skies, the birds of the air and fish of the sea, humans and their animal companions, God placed a period. In the beginning, God introduced an end.

According to the writer of Genesis, human sin forced God to set limits on human beings. No longer would we enjoy the bounty of the Garden of Eden. Nor would we live forever: "You are dust, and to dust you shall return" (Gen 3:19b). There is no side stepping God's intent, no softening the blow. Only God lasts forever. The rest of us die. Our bodies either wear out or give out. Our lungs cease breathing. Our hearts quit beating. Our brains stop thinking. And we die.

Since that same beginning, humans have pretended the period at the end of the sentence didn't exist. We have devised all sorts of schemes to cope with the unwelcome fact of death. The ancients were buried with food and money, sometimes even servants, so they would not be hungry

Sincerely Dead

or impoverished or alone on their journey. We spend billions of dollars each year to medically prolong life as long as possible, hoping to hold death at bay. Even Norman Bates, the twisted innkeeper in *Psycho*, shares our denial, alternately imagining his "sincerely dead" mother to be alive and that he was her.

Please do not misunderstand. I take no delight in the fact of death. I do not gleefully drop the last shovel of dirt on a loved one's casket and turn away: "That's that." The fact of death does not deny the grief that follows it. That we die is incontrovertible. That we grieve the dead is incontrovertible, as well. But death and our response to it are different things.

That is why we need to make a distinction between *death* and *grief*. If it seems I make my case too starkly, too harshly, it is because everything in the world conspires against that distinction. No one lives forever. Not Lisa's grandmother. Not King Tut. Not Elvis Presley. We miss them, grieve them, long for them for the rest of our lives, but that missing/grieving/longing occurs only because death is so real, so final, so complete.

Scripture is replete with references to death, almost preoccupied with the subject. Death is punishment for sin (Gen 3:19). Death is the last enemy (1 Cor 15:26). Death silences our song (Psalm 115:17). Jesus weeps in the face of death (John 11:35). In fact, Jesus himself died. Completely. Finally. Sincerely. That is why his resurrection is such a game-changing event. "Why do you look for the living among the dead?" the empty-tomb-topping angel wondered (Luke 24:5). Even those who witnessed the vacant grave couldn't quite believe it.

Jesus himself is silent on the subject of what death was like; he had more pressing matters to consider. But we wonder about it. Is it like sleep? Are the dead immediately caught up in the air with Christ? Do they wait patiently for his return? Because we cannot know the particulars of death, we must simply trust what we have been told, that the dead are alive in Christ.

There are individuals or families in every congregation who make ministry a particular joy, who make all the work worth it. Aaron and Alexis were two of those people.

Aaron was a smart and funny man, joyful and generous. He was a shrewd businessman who generously shared his wisdom with our congregation's leadership and administration. Alexis was the consummate cookie-baking, storytelling, finger-painting mom, devoted to her three little boys and all of their scabby-kneed little boy friends. Aaron and Alexis were generous with their affection, their time, their wisdom, and their treasure. Just thinking about them makes me smile.

I also know that they had suffered incredible sorrow in their life. My pastoral predecessor and members of the parish had shared the story with me—a story that left scars on everyone who experienced it.

Some years before I knew them, Aaron and Alexis' young daughter Maggie had died unexpectedly in her sleep. They had tucked Maggie into bed one night, warm as toast. When they went to wake her the next morning, her body was cold as ice. The autopsy revealed the cause—a heart defect that could have been repaired in infancy, had it been detected. But no one caught it. And a little girl died.

On the day of the funeral, as the liturgy was about to begin, Aaron and Alexis whispered in the pastor's ear, asking if they could see Maggie one last time before the funeral began. The organist lifted her fingers from the keys, and a church full of grieving mourners sat silently as the funeral director lifted the casket lid. Maggie's mother had been clutching the frayed and faded pink baby blanket under which Maggie had died. She and Aaron unfolded the blanket and laid it gently over Maggie's lifeless body. Later they said, "We needed to tuck her in one last time." Arms around each other's waists, they leaned into her casket, gazing into her beautiful face one last time. They each kissed a no-longer-rosy cheek and nodded at the funeral director, "You can close it now."

I had heard other stories about Maggie's death, too. Stories about multiple and well-meaning attempts to force Maggie's parents to take legal action against the pediatrician who had missed the heart defect that had killed her.

"They should have sued that guy for all he was worth," someone told me.

"If that idiot had been paying attention, Maggie wouldn't have died," another said.

"Somebody should have been punished for that. I can't believe they let it go."

Aaron, Alexis, and I had never spoken directly about Maggie's death, but they knew that I knew. I wondered how these well-rehearsed, harsh, and still-fresh sentiments from parishioners had been received by Maggie's parents. They were not angry or litigious. They were kind and hopeful and full of life.

Aaron and Alexis dropped by the church office one morning and we fell into conversation by the coffee pot. Our conversation turned to the recent death of a teenager in our community. We knew both the deceased and the driver. A high school girl had been killed in a car driven by a newly licensed young man. It was a completely preventable accident caused by inexperience and bravado. It was a tragedy of monumental proportions, a trauma that nearly destroyed both families.

After a thorough investigation, no charges were filed in the accident. But the girl's parents were not satisfied. Her parents were deeply, almost pathologically angry. They wrote letters to the editor. They vandalized the young man's home. They shouted insults from the stands as he played football on Friday nights. They filed lawsuit after lawsuit after lawsuit. They wanted to destroy the young driver for taking their daughter's life, however unintentionally.

Their unabated anger and vicious attacks left all of us in shock. It also prompted me to ask Aaron and Alexis about their experience, their reaction to Maggie's unnecessary death. My questions were clumsy and probably too personal. But I hoped they might share a shred of wisdom that would make sense of the anger that drove other parents who also had suffered a daughter's death.

"Were you angry after Maggie died?" I asked. "Did you think about suing? What do you think of what's happening with the young driver's family?"

Aaron drew his wallet out of his back pocket, pulled a faded photograph from one of the compartments. "This is Maggie. I look at this picture every day. She would be fifteen now, pretty as her mother.

"And no, I'm not angry. Wasn't then either. What good would it do? But, God, I miss her."

Alexis laid her hand on his knee, trained her eyes on my face. "Not a day goes by that I don't miss her. But she's dead. Too soon, but she's dead. Being angry wouldn't bring her back, and a lawsuit wouldn't make it hurt any less."

Aaron continued, "We talked to the doctor. He knows what happened and it nearly killed him. Why make it worse?"

A long pause.

Then he said, "I feel so bad for the driver of that car. But I feel worse for that girl's parents. I wish they weren't so angry. But I guess being mad

Daily Life

at somebody is easier for them than waking up every day knowing their daughter is dead."

The Apostle Paul writes, "We do not want you to be uninformed, brothers and sisters, about those who have died, so that you may not grieve as those do who have no hope" (1 Thess 4:13). In other words, we grieve, but we grieve differently from those who do not believe in Jesus Christ. Note that Paul does not prohibit grieving, or even criticize it. Of course we grieve, sometimes bitterly, but not because we are afraid or hopeless. We grieve so deeply because we love so deeply, not because we have no hope. In our sorrow, we are grateful for all the dead whom we have been privileged to love, and in our gratitude, we recognize the depth of our loss.

Thus, for Christians, the occasion of death is not only an occasion for sorrow, but also for praise.

That is why, at the bedside of one who is dying, we pray:

> God our creator, you called into being this fragile life, which had seemed to us so full of promise. Give to *name*, whom we commit to your care, abundant life in your presence, and to us who grieve, courage to bear our loss; through Jesus Christ, our Savior and Lord. Amen.[2]

That is why, as we welcome worshippers to the funeral, we begin with this invitation:

> Welcome in the name of Jesus, the Savior of the world.
> We are gathered to worship,
> to proclaim Christ crucified and risen,
> to remember before God our *sister/brother* _____,
> to give thanks for *her/his* life,
> to commend *her/him* to our merciful redeemer,
> and to comfort one another in our grief.[3]

That is why at funerals we choke our way through the familiar hymn:

> Were they to take our house, goods, honor, child or spouse,
> though life be wrenched away, they cannot win the day.[4]

---

2. "Commendation of the Dying," *Evangelical Lutheran Worship Pastoral Care*, 214.
3. "Funeral Liturgy," *Evangelical Lutheran Worship Pew Edition*, 279.
4. Luther, "A Mighty Fortress Is Our God," *Evangelical Lutheran Worship*, #504.

That is why we stand at the grave and announce, "Death has been swallowed up in victory" (1 Cor 15:54).

That is why in the Apostles' Creed we confess to faith in "the communion of saints," that great gathering of God's people living and dead who continue in relationship with God and one another beyond the confines of time and space.

We do not deny death. We know it to be absolute, undeniable, reliable, sincere. But we also keep death in its proper place, knowing that it is, after all, only death. It is not ultimate. It is not the last word.

It is God's love for us that is ultimate, enduring, most sincere. God's love alone sustains us. In this life, and the next.

Daily Life

Sincerely Dead Questions for Discussion

1. What is the central dilemma posed by this essay?

2. Many congregations offer a "celebration of life" rather than a funeral at the time of death. What are the pitfalls and merits of hosting a "celebration" rather than a "funeral?"

3. How do we acknowledge both the gift of life and its necessary end, without obsessing about or obfuscating either?

A Last Word

The last word is often the most coveted.

To throw a "So there!" over your shoulder as you flee the scene of a marital fight. To make the clarifying point in a meeting, leaving others speechless at your wisdom. To silence detractors with a stinging rebuke, robbing them of the opportunity to fire again. Too often the last word is a harsh one, a competitive one, an intentionally painful one.

Last words can also be amusing, as evidenced by the *Car Talk* guys on National Public Radio, who have compiled a list of hilarious last words:

"Does your dog bite?"

"I wonder where the mother bear is?"

"What does this button do?"

Last words are for headstones. And jokes. And divorces.

There will be no definitive last word in these pages, no sage bon mot to summarize all that has come before, or that leaves the reader dumbfounded by the writer's wit and whimsy.

The last words belong to you, the parish pastor, the council president, the seminary student, the Sunday school teacher. My stories beg your own.

Where have you struggled to see God at work?

How do you reconcile the bracing "fact" of the church with Jesus' prayer for it?

What questions will you ask God when invited to come up higher?

Thank you for the privilege of walking beside you for a while, swapping stories and sharing the load. I trust you have found your stories well-stewarded.

Bibliography

Bonhoeffer, Dietrich. *Life Together: A Discussion of Christian Fellowship.* New York: Harper, 1954.
Evangelical Lutheran Church in America. *Evangelical Lutheran Worship.* Leaders' Edition. Minneapolis, MN: Augsburg Fortress Publishers, 2006.
———. *Evangelical Lutheran Worship.* Pastoral Care Edition. Minneapolis, MN: Augsburg Fortress Publishers, 2006.
———. *Evangelical Lutheran Worship.* Pew Edition. Minneapolis, MN: Augsburg Fortress Publishers, 2006.
———. *Occasional Services for the Assembly.* Minneapolis, MN: Augsburg Fortress Publishers, 2006.
Kolb, Robert, and Timothy J. Wengert, eds. *The Book of Concord: The Confessions of the Evangelical Lutheran Church.* Minneapolis, MN: Fortress Press, 2000.
MGM Studios. *The Wizard of Oz.* 1939.

www.ingramcontent.com/pod-product-compliance
Lightning Source LLC
Chambersburg PA
CBHW051104160426
43193CB00010B/1303